HIRE POWER

BY **RIKKA** BRANDON

Everything Lumber and Building Materials Leaders Need To Know To Hire Better in Any Market

HIRE POWER

What Lumber and Building Materials Leaders Need To Know To Hire
Better In Any Market

ISBN: 978-0-578-74864-1

The Brandon Group, Moorhead, MN

BISAC: Business & Economics / Human Resources
& Personnel Management

Printed in the United States of America.

DISCLAIMER

This book is designed to provide information on hiring only. This information is provided and sold with the knowledge that the publisher and author do not offer any legal or other professional advice. In the case of a need for any such expertise consult with the appropriate professional. This book does not contain all information available on the subject. This book has not been created to be specific to any individual's or organizations' situation or needs. Every effort has been made to make this book as accurate as possible. However, there may be typographical and or content errors. Therefore, this book should serve only as a general guide and not as the ultimate source of subject information. This book contains information that might be dated and is intended only to educate and entertain. The author and publisher shall have no liability or responsibility to any person or entity regarding any loss or damage incurred, or alleged to have incurred, directly or indirectly, by the information contained in this book. You hereby agree to be bound by this disclaimer or you may return this book within the guarantee period for a full refund. In the interest of full disclosure, this book contains affiliate links that might pay the author or publisher a commission upon any purchase from the company. While the author and publisher take no responsibility for the business practices of these companies and or the performance of any product or service, the author or publisher has used the product or service and makes a recommendation in good faith based on that experience.

HIRE POWER

To Bill Lee, who told me I should be the person to write the book on recruiting and hiring in the LBM Industry. Without your nudge this may not have happened! Thank you for the encouragement!

To Chris, there aren't enough words. Best. Husband. Ever. is a good start though.

To Carsten and Tegan, You're (still) my inspiration to strive and my reason to stay present in the moment. I'm so glad I'm your Mom. You're two of the coolest kids - ever.

PRAISE
for Rikka Brandon

"In the LBM industry, hiring has perplexed many hiring managers and companies, oftentimes leading to less than satisfactory results.

I have had the pleasure of both knowing Rikka personally and working with her for several years, and have watched her endeavor to transform the way that we as an industry think about hiring. Rikka is truly a visionary in her field, and believes that the psychology and strategy of hiring are not exclusive of one another.

She has the unique ability to quantify and qualify what may be of benefit to you and your company, even when you may be struggling for clarity of thought. Adept at drawing out the "WIMI" (what is most important), she then will collaborate to construct a strategy, then advise and coach on the tactical process to ensure highest results.

Perhaps most impressive about Rikka is her ability to succinctly analyze information and trends as our industry continues to evolve, and then pivot and adapt strategy to suit the framework of the operating environment. Never one to let you rest on your laurels, she will push you to succeed — and then celebrate your successes with you.

I think you will learn much from this book; I know that I did. And if you are fortunate enough to connect with Rikka — do it! She is an advocate for LBM, and will be for you and your company!"

— DENA CORDOVA-JACK
Executive Vice President
Mountain States Lumber and Building Materials Dealers Assosication

"Rikka Brandon is a fantastic resource! We call her for the really hard ones, and 9 times out of 10 we get a winner. We especially like the fact that she is real. She hits it hard from the start and doesn't quit until she's exhausted every possibility. If she can't find what we need, she tells us straight away rather than stringing the search along. Rikka is extremely energetic and enthusiastic (think Energizer Bunny). She gets the job done, and it's fun along the way. Fun to deal with, strives for immediate results, keeps us updated constantly. They are unique to our industry and know the lingo. We have also been working together long enough that they know our culture and really care about finding the right person."

— **DOUG SHOREY**
Vice President of HR
American Building Supply

"Rikka is my "go-to-girl" for rock-solid recruiting, interviewing, hiring, and coaching advice! The depth of her knowledge and experience is second to none in the LBM industry. Unlike many recruiters, she is always willing to share her little-known tips, techniques, and tricks to help anyone hire better AND smarter. Rikka gives it straight up, straight forward in a warm, approachable manner that makes every conversation a pleasure.

In short, she absolutely is the top of her profession!"

— **THEA DUDLEY**
The Leading LBM Credit Expert
Owner, Pocket Protectors LLC

"You don't know what you don't know." This was the thought that came to mind when I read my first article by Rikka Brandon. I thought I had above-average skills when it came to interviewing and hiring, but I quickly learned that I still had a lot to learn. Since that time, I have read dozens of her articles and developed a professional relationship with her that has taken my knowledge and abilities beyond the next level.

Rikka has taught me that recruiting and hiring isn't a process but more of a well-planned surgical procedure. She takes a comprehensive approach that starts with an in-depth analysis of the needs to establish a clear definition to best position the opportunity for a more efficient and effective candidate list. From there, the recruiting, interviewing, hiring, and onboarding process is a choreographed unity to achieve a common goal and provide the greatest benefits to all parties involved.

Rikka's passion and commitment for growing and building this industry is second to none, and her energy identifies and inspires the top talent. She has the versatility to teach best practices for every step of the procedure or her services are for hire. Rikka's talents and expertise go above and beyond just interviewing and hiring, and she teaches the great benefits of a well-established recruiting and hiring plan."

— P. BRETT THORNE
The Lumberjack
Building The Future Podcast
Thorne Lumber

TABLE OF CONTENTS

Introduction
to the HIRE

POWER

METHOD

Few things can change the trajectory of an LBM business more than hiring.

One of the most vexing things about hiring (and hiring well) is that there are just so many variables that could be causing issues. Pair that with the fact that we're dealing with people on both sides of the hiring equation and you add in other subjective and emotional considerations. As with most things worth doing it takes a strong desire to "figure it out" and a willingness to put the effort in to gain the education and experience you'll need to succeed.

However, your success is very closely tied to the level of performance you get from your team members. With a strong and reliable team you experience higher profit margins, increased sales, and the opportunity to expand into new products, services, and markets. If your team consists of more "best that applied" than "best in class" you'll find yourself spending more time training, managing, and redirecting your employees to ensure your business is moving in the right direction. It's exhausting.

However, as you already know - Hiring is complicated. That's why it's helpful to have a friendly guide to show you the path, a recognized expert in LBM recruiting and hiring. A Guru, if you will. Now, you may think of the term Guru as a spiritual or "woo-woo" term, but both Wikipedia and Merriam-Webster agree that it's more than just that.

A teacher and especially
INTELLECTUAL GUIDE

INTRODUCTION

It was with this understanding of the term Guru that I decided to name my executive search firm Building Gurus. I thought it would show that I could guide and advise my clients on the recruiting and hiring journey. Now, as I start to do more training, coaching, and advising it feels even more fitting.

I love recruiting. I love the strategy of search, the thrill of the hunt, and most of all I love finding the perfect fit for my clients and my candidates. I'm excited to share the tricks and tips I've learned over the years as I've worked with Fortune 100 companies all the way down to helping solopreneurs hire their first employee. I've spent almost 20 years helping LBM and Building Products Manufacturers and Distributors find and hire the best talent for their openings. In that time, I've worked on thousands of searches for hundreds of companies, interviewed well over 10,000 industry professionals, and placed over 600 employees with my clients. It was through all of these experiences that I developed and refined the Hire Power Method. It's not a step-by-step guide, that simply doesn't work with something as complex and fluid as hiring. Instead, the goal is to educate and empower you so you can start hiring better and continue to improve in the years to come.

The LBM industry has hiring challenges, but it also has HUGE opportunities. If you decide that your business is going to "win" at the war for talent - I couldn't be more excited to help you achieve that goal.

To that end, we need to start where you are right now. I know, this isn't fun or exciting (and frankly, you may have been looking the other way for quite awhile). Think of this as a bit like dieting. We need to understand where we are to see how far we have come in the future. Also, like diet and exercise, this isn't something that can be fixed by spending a few hard core hours working on it and then "checking it off" your to do list. You need to gain knowledge and then consistently apply that knowledge, and see what works so you can do more of it.

Once you have an understanding of where you're starting from, we'll start looking at each step of the recruiting, and hiring process. Section two will help you get clear, and make sure you're being realistic. In section three you'll learn how to get more qualified applicants. Section four is when you'll learn how to interview like a pro and extend offers that get accepted. It's also where you'll learn what to do when your offer gets declined, or your new hire disappoints.

When You **KNOW BETTER**, You **DO BETTER**

This book is full of guidance and helpful tips, but there is even more help available. If you see the icon below (the screwdriver and wrench), it means that there is more information and related downloads in your free bonus the LBM Hiring Toolkit.

 You can download your copy of the Hiring Toolkit, plus bonus resources for FREE at www.HirePowerBook.com/LBMtoolkit.

Hopefully, your hiring problems are simple and easy to solve. But, if you feel like you need an expert to guide you, be sure to check the back of the book for ways we can work together to help you find, hire, and keep the people you need to move from potential to profit in your business.

Just so we are all on the same page, let's review some common recruiting terms I will be using:

Clarity: Getting clear about what you need and why.

Compensation: Compensation is different than salary. Salary is part of compensation, but compensation packages include commission, bonuses, car allowance, perks, etc.

Attraction: Promoting your job openings in a way that results in the candidate actively reaching out to you, usually by applying to your job postings.

Sourcing: The process of seeking out and finding people (usually online) who have the experience you are looking for. Generally, the "research" part of the recruiting process.

Recruiting: Promoting your job openings in a way that involves you reaching out and starting the conversation with people you've targeted.

Search: What third-party recruiters refer to when we talk about the whole process of sourcing and recruiting candidates for openings.

Candidates: Another name for job applicants.

Okay, let's get down to business.

section one

FOUNDATIONS
for
SUCCESS

HIRE POWER

You already know that when you know better, you do better.

Unfortunately, there aren't very many classes that teach you how to understand what's working and not working in your recruiting and hiring process. So you're stuck best-guessing what needs to change and in what way. Plus, hiring is always important, but it often only gets moved to a priority position when you're suddenly dealing with an unexpected resignation or a mass influx of business and realize you're dropping the ball more than you like.

To move ahead of your competitors, you need to move beyond the status quo. You need to make time to think about recruiting, selection, and retention — before it's an emergency. You need to recognize that hiring well is a complex mix of psychology, marketing, and sales. It's a complicated game and to play it and win requires a will to succeed.

I'm excited to be your guide as you learn how to assess your current recruiting and hiring processes and start making changes that deliver results.

It's not a walk in the park to build successful recruiting and hiring processes for all the roles on your team. But, in the words of Mae West, "I never said it would be easy, I only said it would be worth it."

> "I never said it would be
> **EASY,**
> I only said it would be
> **WORTH IT."**

chapter one

Your *Employer* BRAND

Every LBM and building products company has a reputation — good, bad, or somewhere in the middle. It could include thoughts about your products, services, branding, market positioning, leadership, team members, history, and more.

However, your business has another reputation that you're likely less aware of and almost certainly give less thought and attention to. This is your Employer Brand. It's also referred to as your Talent Brand or People Brand. This is the reputation your actions and dealings with current and past employees have created.

Employer Brands exist and impact your hiring success — even if you haven't given them any thought or been strategic about them.

13

Hopefully, you've acted in a way you're proud of in your dealings with applicants and employees, so you've created a strong foundation for your Employer Brand. Unfortunately, not all hiring managers or companies think about the long-term ramifications of not being prepared for interviews, leaving candidates hanging for days or weeks waiting for an answer about next steps, and failing to recognize and appreciate the contributions of their employees. For those of you in this situation, you may need to work to repair the damage that's already been done. But, the good news is now that you know better, you'll do better. Right?

As an industry we're feeling the ramifications of the loss of mid-level managers in the Great Recession when we try to fill our senior leadership roles; we're dealing with an aging workforce and the reality of how much knowledge and customer information they have in their heads that we haven't effectively captured. Pair that with our stumbling attempts to be more appealing to the generations entering the workforce, and you understand why you post a job opening and feel underwhelmed with the applicants. Even with the massive disruption in the talent market caused by COVID-19, many LBM dealers have found themselves unable to find the caliber of talent they want to hire. These extenuating circumstances have led smart and forward-thinking hiring managers and companies to recognize the importance of their Employer Brand.

Without a positive Employer Brand, hiring and retaining the best employees becomes challenging and expensive. Your LBM business needs strong employees in the yard, in the office, in sales roles, and of course in leadership positions. The best way to attract and recruit the talent you need is by giving them the impression that your company is a great place to work. The way you get great employees to stay is by *being* a great place to work.

Your Employer Brand or reputation derives from numerous decisions and actions you or your company make. From how you treat applicants and interviewees to creating a workplace where your employees feel engaged, challenged, and rewarded all play into how your company is seen in the marketplace and can greatly impact how potential employees view your company.

. . . .

Harvard Business Review's research found that the **top three factors that contribute most to a reputation as a bad place to work** are concerns about job security, dysfunctional teams, and poor leadership. The **top three factors associated with a good reputation as an employer** are stability, opportunities for career growth, and the ability to work with a top-notch team.

. . . .

I'm a fan of working smart and hard. So, don't feel like you need to start from scratch to build your employer brand. Look to your customer-facing branding and marketing materials to create the foundation for your Employer Brand. As you move forward with making decisions about how to deal with your applicants, interviewees, and employees, keep the power of your Employer Brand and "what's in it for them" top of mind so you can start making informed decisions and making smart moves as decisions come up.

As with all marketing, building a strong Employer Brand is about creating a compelling narrative. **It's about deciding how you want your organization to be perceived in the market and then being intentional with your actions and messaging to ensure you are viewed that way.** One of the most effective ways to get your message out to the world is by showcasing your employees; they are the best way for you to demonstrate that you walk your talk and that your Employer Brand isn't just a "good story." By becoming intentional about what you want the world to know and featuring your employees on social media, in videos, or in articles, you're taking control of the message — which is especially important in these days of social media, Glassdoor, and other feedback opportunities that limit the control you have over your own reputation.

The good news is that simply by reading this you've created an awareness you may not have had before, and it will impact your decisions and actions going forward, and even small or simple changes can improve your Employer Brand.

If you want to turn your Employer Brand into a competitive edge, read on.

WHY IT MATTERS

HOW NOT INVESTING IN YOUR EMPLOYER BRAND IS GOING TO COST YOU

Choosing not to focus on your Employer Brand is going to cost you — and not in a general, intangible way. It will cost you (over and over) in time, money, and results. Although these examples are for companies with poor reputations, the same challenges apply to misdirected, misunderstood, or outdated Employer Brands.

⚡ MORE APPLICANTS

Companies with a favorable reputation can get up to TWICE as many applications as companies with negative reputations. Yes, some of them will be unqualified, but if you get two good candidates for each 100 applications, wouldn't you rather weed through 200 resumes and have four quality candidates to choose from? As a third-party recruiter, we strive to provide three to five qualified and interested candidates to our clients so they can make an informed choice without being overwhelmed by eight to 10 interviews.

⚡ FEWER DECLINED OFFERS

According to 3BL Media's corporate reputation survey, if unemployed, nearly 70% of American males said they would NOT join a company with a bad reputation. When it comes to female Americans, the percentage jumps to 86%. Just think of that: two out of three Americans would rather be *unemployed* than work for a company that doesn't have a good reputation.

⚡ INCREASED COST TO HIRE

According to Harvard Business Review's research, it costs a company with a poor reputation 10% more per hire. With an average pay of $47,230, that leads to nearly $5,000 per hire than a company with a good reputation. Multiply that by the number of employees you have. Ouch.

⚡ MORE MONEY ISN'T ENOUGH TO GET THEM TO SAY YES

The minimum increase in pay required by employed applicants to accept a role with a company that has a poor reputation is 10%, and even *with* a 10% increase in pay, only 28% of them would be tempted to join a company with a bad reputation. That's less than one out of three.

However, when top candidates want to work for you, it has the opposite effect. Your cost to hire drops drastically — by around 43%. This is because there is less to overcome when trying to get to yes on your offer than if you're dealing with a poor reputation. Your HR team, recruiters, and hiring managers are able to focus more on screening and selecting than selling through the often intangible obstacles created by your poor employer reputation.

Who is responsible for employer branding?

I get it, it's easy to hope this is someone else's responsibility. But, chances are if you're reading this book, you are responsible for it.

At the strategic level, your leadership team (making sure that HR has a seat at the table) is responsible for prioritizing and funding your employer branding efforts. Of course, with all things it varies by the size of your company and the organization's structure. I firmly believe that the highest level of leadership needs to understand and be "bought in" to the ROI a strong employer brand can bring so they'll apply their authority and financial power to ensure that this isn't something "important" that doesn't get attention until it's "urgent." Competitive and forward-thinking leaders will recognize that in the long run, investing in their Employer Brand will yield a tremendous ROI in future years.

The reality is that you can craft the message and position your organization, but the "success" of your employer branding is largely determined by your employees. Your Employer Brand or reputation is closely tied to the experiences of your employees and what they say about your organization and working there. If you're saying you're family-friendly, but Glassdoor is full of reviews saying that you micromanage PTO, it's not only off message, it makes your company look like it's trying to pull a bait and switch.

WARNING: The LBM industry is full of family-owned companies. Be mindful that if you promote being family friendly that your flexibility and understanding extends to people who aren't part of the founding family. We've all known companies that allow behavior from people in the family that wouldn't be tolerated by other employees.

Or perhaps you talk about promoting from within, but you can't showcase anyone who actually has been promoted from entry level to management; it leaves candidates wondering if it's really true. So, the responsibility of ensuring your desired Employer Brand matches reality rests squarely on the shoulders of your leadership, managers, and HR. They need to work to ensure that they understand what employees appreciate and value about working for your organization and what they'd like to see change. If you don't have a healthy company culture and work environment — work to fix that first. It's no good to pour water into a bucket that's full of holes.

chapter two

Take A
Recruiting
AUDIT

Now we're getting to the fun part! If you've ever heard me speak, you know that I get excited about the impact great recruiting and hiring can have on a business, not to mention the work-life balance of managers and executives.

I firmly believe that well-executed recruiting and hiring strategies will drive some of the strongest ROI you'll see in your business.

Now, when you've been stuck settling for the "best that applied," that may feel like a bold claim (or a delusion). But keep in mind, companies don't often pay my fees unless the position is very tough to fill, so it makes sense we'd have a different view.

I'm excited to show you what's possible and help you start to see how recruiting can drive ROI.

But first, we have to understand what is working and what needs improvement. Don't worry, I'm not going to ask you to dig into spreadsheets to find data (unless you're into that sort of thing — then go for it!).

Recruiting Audit Questions

This is a series of simple questions that are designed to help you get clear about what is working well in your recruiting and hiring process and what areas need some more attention. Use the lines below each question as a place to capture to-dos, notes, and anything else that will help you take action later.

Do you take time to review the job description to ensure the role and responsibilities are still accurate due to changes in technology, systems, and your business needs and direction BEFORE you post the job?

_____

_____

_____

_____

Are you able to clearly define the daily, weekly, or monthly activities and expected results for each role before you hire for it? This doesn't mean you're hiring a sales person to increase sales by 10%; it means you know what actions they need to take consistently to get your desired results.

_____

_____

_____

_____

Do you consistently communicate these expectations to candidates before offering them a position?

_____

_____

_____

_____

If you didn't feel confident answering these (which most readers won't, if they're being honest), you'll want to pay attention to the upcoming section on Clarity.

Do you feel confident that your compensation package is competitive and compelling? Is your confidence based on research and facts?

_____

_____

_____

_____

Do you often have applicants pull out of the process, job offers declined, no shows, or turnover in the first 90 days for a better opportunity?

_____

_____

_____

_____

Do you often feel disappointed in your new hires?

_____

_____

_____

_____

Do you use vendors, freelancers, independent contractors, or any non-W2-type of employment to meet your business needs?

_____

_____

_____

_____

If any of these resonated with you, be sure to pay attention in the upcoming Reality section to learn how to ensure your compensation is (actually) competitive and you're being realistic with your expectations.

Do you often get unsolicited strong candidates or referrals?

_____

_____

_____

_____

Do you get enough quality and quantity of applicants from your current recruiting efforts?

_____

_____

_____

_____

Does it feel like you're just not getting in front of the right people?

_____

_____

_____

_____

Does it feel like you're in front of the right people, but they just aren't applying?

_____

_____

_____

_____

Are you doing anything beyond posting a job ad?

_____

_____

_____

_____

If any of these questions indicated an area for improvement, you'll enjoy the Attract and Recruit section.

Do you have an established hiring and vetting process you trust?

_____

_____

_____

_____

Do you use anything other than interviews in your selection process?

_____

_____

_____

_____

Do you feel like you sometimes get fooled by "smooth talkers" in the interview process?

_____

_____

_____

_____

Do you lose candidates during the interview process? Or perhaps they apply but you can never get an interview scheduled, or they pull themselves out of consideration (before you've rejected them).

_____

_____

_____

_____

You'll find the answers to challenges like this in Interviews and Offers.

Good work. Congrats on completing the recruiting audit. (Oh, you just skimmed over it, did you?) Well, if you want to build a business that delivers the results you want and a better work-life balance — it's worth spending 15 minutes to get clear about what *really* needs your attention.

Go ahead, go back and do it. I'll wait.

Okay, chances are you hadn't even considered that some of these things could be negatively impacting your recruiting and hiring success. Just remember, knowledge is power. Now that you know better, you can do better. The answer to these problems is in your hands. Feel free to jump ahead and check out the info, but if you're serious about figuring this out for the long haul you'll want to understand the process and psychology from the beginning until the end.

PRO TIP *Don't let overwhelm stop you from talking action. Small steps can result in big changes. The worst thing you can do is keep looking the other way, hoping it will get better. Just pick one thing to work on. It could be your biggest pain point or something easy. But, move forward.*

section two

CLARITY
and
REALITY

HIRE POWER

Making a great hire doesn't start when you're face to face with a potential recruit. It begins with upfront planning, a process that I call, "Getting Clear."

Clarity is the effort you put in before you even post a job ad or start interviewing. By determining, ahead of time, why you need this role and what its responsibilities will be, what results you expect from the new hire in this role, and what activity levels they will need to maintain to get those results, you can create a stronger job description that sets expectations and objectives clearly upfront. This will guide not only those applying for the position, but the way in which you recruit, interview, and, ultimately, make your final decision.

The first step to avoiding bad hires?
GETTING CLEAR

Without upfront clarity, you can't write a job description that is compelling to the right people and ensures the wrong people to self-select out. If you've been posting job descriptions, instead of job ads, you're likely getting very few qualified applicants. That means you're either not getting many applicants at all (because it's not compelling) or you're getting a lot of unqualified applicants because they just skimmed it and figured they'd apply. Both of these results lead to you losing faith that you're going to find a qualified person to hire. That often leads to trying to "make it work."

Take, for example, hiring for a new sales rep, either to replace a departing team member or to add more capacity to your sales team.

You know you need someone who can go out into the field and see customers as your yard's face around town.

So, you post an ad for an outside sales person.

But without that clarity, and subsequent clear and compelling job ad, the applications pouring in aren't in the ballpark of what you need.

The first person to respond is an inside sales person.

You think to yourself: *Well, maybe that could work! It would probably be cheaper, right? Yeah, I think they could just call the customers. After all, I still have other sales people to see customers in the field or maybe they are itching for the chance to become an outside sales person. I could train them … oh yeah, that would be good. I'd get someone I can train to do it my way, and I wouldn't have to pay them so much. This seems promising!*

DING.

The second response comes in. This person is a marketing manager.

You think: *Oh, I've been thinking about hiring a marketing manager. We need to have a concentrated marketing effort. Wow, look at that. They worked for XYZ company, so they must be sharp. I wonder if they could do a blend of outside sales and marketing? That would be awesome. We could quit paying that firm so much every month and bring it back in house … oh yeah, that has potential to work!*

DING.

The third response comes from someone with experience in outside sales but in a completely different industry.

You think: *Look at that. They are used to making 80 calls a week on customers. Imagine the potential of someone reaching out to over 300 new targeted leads each month. Wow, that would be amazing! I realize that we sell building materials and their experience is medical devices, but if you can sell something, you can sell anything, right? If they converted 10%, that would be 30 new*

34

customers a month. We'd have to add customer service reps just to take care of all the new business!

DING.

Without clarity from the get-go, you're (a) limiting your ability to attract and engage the right talent, (b) weeding through applicants who clearly aren't a fit for the role, and (c) considering these unqualified applicants and making justifications for how they might fit. These mental gymnastics will lead to a bad hire that costs you more time and headaches down the road. Having clarity ahead of time will allow you to attract and engage more qualified candidates (more on this in Attract and Recruit), and it will make it easy for candidates to realize it's not the right role for them so you can spend less time reviewing unqualified applications.

chapter three

How All GREAT HIRES Start

All great hires start with you and your ability to clarify what you need and a recognition of your realities: what you can spend and what you expect the new hire to do.

Clarity doesn't always mean you know exactly who you're going to hire, but it does mean you know exactly what you need and why.

As a recruiter who has spent most my career working on a pay-for-performance contract, I learned early on that if an employer can't clearly describe what they need, I am very unlikely to find someone they want.

If there isn't clarity, as a hiring manager/owner you won't work on a search.

Without clarity, you're setting yourself up for an employee who doesn't fit the role — and the subsequent time, monetary, and emotional investment that follows.

You're the one who will be stuck training (and re-training) the employee, managing and likely reprimanding them. When it doesn't work out, you're the one accepting their resignation (maybe happily). In the worst cases, you're the one who has to fire them.

Clarity is an investment of your time and energy. It requires that someone who understands the business realities determines what the business needs.

This investment of time upfront has a *huge* ROI. For every hour you invest upfront, you will save yourself at least ten hours of "tail chasing" down the road. When you are clear about your business needs and what you expect, you don't waste time chasing "what ifs" or making up reasons it could work.

Clarity ensures you're able to:

⚡ Articulate a business need for the position.

⚡ Set and communicate clear performance expectations for the new hire.

⚡ Set performance expectations that you both agree to — before spending a dollar on payroll.

⚡ Focus on what you need, not what could be. (This is where optimism can end up being very costly).

⚡ Understand the return on investment and value of the position.

Once you are clear about what you need to hire, you will:

⚡ Create a great job description (and ultimately a great job ad to attract your ideal hire).

⚡ Weed out people who aren't a good fit; no more hemming and hawing.

⚡ Stop wasting money, time, and energy.

⚡ Know what you need to see a return on investment in the position.

⚡ Build the framework to guide your recruiting strategy and interview process.

Four Questions for Clarity

Before you hire anyone, you need to be able to answer these questions with a solid YES!

⚡ **Is it worth it?**
Is it worth the time, cost, and energy required to hire someone? Will the end result make it worth the effort?

⚡ **Can you clearly set expectations for activities and results?**
Can you give them a statement of expectations to agree to and sign before they accept your offer?

⚡ **Are you ready, willing, and able to train and support them for the next three months?**
Even if they can hit the ground running, they won't know your products, processes, and procedures.

⚡ **How long can you "carry" this person before they need to start paying for themselves?**
The reality is, most sales people take four to six months before they start covering their payroll costs. Can you afford to wait that long?

I get it. This is a LOT of work. It's not easy to get clear. It feels like there are too many variables to consider. But, trust me. It's much easier to get clear before you hire someone than regret it when you have an under-performing employee whom you're paying to disappoint you.

NOT hiring someone is MUCH easier than FIRING them!

WARNING: Many people find that when they actually take the time to go through these steps, it becomes very clear that they aren't actually ready to hire yet. This is what I call working smart, not hard! Now, you know you need to get a bit more clarification before you invest your time, money, and energy into someone and likely end up disappointed in the end.

INSIDER INFO

THINKING ABOUT HIRING A FRIEND OR FAMILY MEMBER?

There's no doubt about it: finding new, high-potential talent to hire can be daunting. A ton of factors are at play beyond just resumes and recommendations. You need to make sure you hire a trustworthy person who learns quickly, does their job well, and gets along beautifully with you and the rest of your staff.

This is why a lot of small or family-owned LBM dealers fall into the same trap: They take the "easiest option," and hire someone they know — a friend, family member, or acquaintance from church. They believe it's much better to bring someone they know on board, rather than a complete stranger.

Does it work? Sometimes. But often, it's a recipe for disaster. How the story unfolds depends on the owner and employee. However, most business owners eventually end up feeling trapped and restricted because of this "easy" hire.

While hiring a neighbor or your college roommate might seem like a no-brainer, it can get messy when it comes time to discipline or fire them. I tell my clients and everyone I discuss hiring with: **Do NOT hire anyone without first imagining what it will be like to fire them.**

To avoid this awkward situation, ask yourself these questions before you approach someone from your immediate circle:

1. **Will I be setting them up to success?**

   Is this role clearly defined? Do we already have someone doing it who can help with training? Do I realistically have the systems and processes set up OR the time to work with them one on one that they'll need to thrive?

2. **Am I willing to let this person go if it doesn't work out?**

   The freedom to take charge, enforce discipline, and accept that an employee isn't a fit is essential to a happy team and well-run business. When you hire a friend, you risk holding back on making the right decision to save their feelings.

3. **Will they be treated like every other staff member, or do I risk favoring them (even subconsciously)?**

   It's easy to give preferential treatment to someone you know personally. Check in with yourself to see if you're *really* willing to treat them like you would any member of your staff.

4. **If they're a friend or family member, will working together affect our relationship outside of the workplace?**

   Should things go south, there will be more fallout than a simple office conversation. Are you ready to handle that? Remember: you might respect your family member or friend deeply, but the workplace presents a completely different environment — one that may not be the right fit for that person.

Reality of Hiring

It's exhausting to try to find and hire great people, especially if you're dealing with applicants pulling themselves out, declined offers, no shows, and underwhelming performance. It can make you feel like you're no good at it and that it's basically a game of chance.

Let's take a closer look. If you've made several successful hires and had one fail, you're doing awesome! After all, you're dealing with people, and they are complex beings that can be impacted at any time by a life change.

A solid long-time employee can have a personal crisis and be unable to focus on work like before.

A works-all-the-time (and loves it) employee might fall in love and suddenly stop working morning to night.

A competitor might offer your star employee a $20,000 pay raise, right as they found out they are expecting … again, and they could *really* use the money.

You might make a decision that they don't agree with.

They might make a decision *you* don't agree with.

Many things can happen; it's not always somebody's fault when an employment relationship ends. Maybe you've been a little hard on yourself, because that's pretty common with managers and leaders.

Still, we've all been in a situation where we could've made a better decision upfront.

Maybe you've been slammed with business, and you realize you need to hire someone NOW. There is NO time to be strategic. So, you post an ad or talk to a couple friends. You quickly hire the first person who expresses interest and seems remotely qualified and easy to work with.

Soon you realize that getting them up to speed is taking more time than it would have just to do the work yourself. Now, you're annoyed with them, but more so with yourself. You screwed up again. You keep this under-performing and mediocre employee because you've decided that their failure is your fault. So, now you haven't reduced your workload by much, but you've upped your costs dramatically. Two years later, they're still with you, because firing people sucks and you're not confident you can do any better next time.

I believe most hiring mistakes are caused by a feeling of scarcity. When you feel like there is no one good out there, it makes it easy to accept sub-par candidates. Unfortunately, it almost always ends with you wasting time and money (and often going through the hiring process again).

There is a silver lining though. Driven, passionate people are naturals at recruiting and hiring. Chances are that you didn't end up in a leadership role because you are happy with the status quo and taking what is given to you. No, you believe in making your own luck, and that smart and hard work can achieve anything. You just don't know how to apply that drive to hiring (yet).

Your feelings of scarcity will go away once you understand how to find like-minded people who are excited by your products and services and engaged in the mission of your company. You will start to build a team of smart and engaged people who can help take your business to the next level.

Before taking that step, however, you need to consider a few more realities.

Assess Your Current Team

If you think it's time to hire and already have an existing team, start with your current people. When you take the time to assess your current team members' capabilities, availability, and desire to perform the work you intend to hire for, you can potentially save yourself a ton of time, effort, and money. Besides, it's always good to be known as a company that "grows their own" by promoting from within. If it feels overwhelming or time-consuming to conduct a SWOT on your team, reach out to a consultant to help you.

Assess Your Financial Reality

Unless you're in the small minority of businesses for whom money is no object, you likely have some financial considerations to keep in mind when adding staff. For many small businesses, payroll is one of the largest expenses on their books. Because of this, it's imperative that you're very clear on what you need and what you can afford.

Technology is rapidly changing how we work and will continue to do so for the foreseeable future. You should be updating job descriptions and your expectations regularly to keep up with how technology is enabling your team to work more efficiently and effectively.

This also means you should consider using vendors, freelancers, contractors, and partners to tackle parts of your business that require special knowledge or skills, but aren't something that warrants a W2 position. Think of your accountant and attorney. Besides marketing and advertising agencies, you can no find graphic designers, blog writers, outbound sales reps, virtual receptionists and more that will be excited to work on your projects.

. . . .

PRO TIP *The next time someone leaves a skilled position, assess the role, see if you can outsource some or all of it and save money on payroll, taxes, and benefits. It won't always be a good move, but it needs to be considered more often by building products companies. Other industries are capitalizing on this, and it can drive results for you too.*

. . . .

Assess How Much You Should Pay for the Position

There are several ways to figure out how much you should pay your new hire.

Use www.salary.com or www.payscale.com to research what similar roles in your area are paying.

. . . .

Make sure your
COMPENSATION matches
your **EXPECTATIONS.**

. . . .

These websites offer a great deal of information and resources for free. Be aware that the information you can access for free is often based on larger markets or U.S. averages. So, if it seems very high (or low) for your area, you probably want to keep researching (or pay for a report).

Contact your local job service or workforce services to see what compensation is for a similar position. They should be able to give you the information you are seeking or direct you to someone who can. For industry-specific information for sales roles, check out the annual LBM Journal salary survey report. You can also check my website BuildingGurus. com; we often have compensation guides available to help you determine what the market is paying now.

Look at job postings for similar positions. Some of them will include compensation details that will give you some insight.

If you still don't have a solid idea, start your interviewing process and ask every candidate what they are expecting the compensation plan to look like. Determine your answer from that information.

If possible, once you have moved through and answered these questions, take a break from it (a reality check, if you will). Come back after a few hours or even a day. Make sure you are being realistic about what you can afford.

chapter four

The **JOB** Description

The job description is one of the most under-utilized tools in the small business toolkit. A well-written job description can serve you for many years. You may need to review and adjust it, but the framework of the role will likely stay very consistent. It is worth the time and effort to do it right.

The job description does much more than just explain a position.

- It's a written statement of the employee's tasks, duties, and responsibilities.
- It establishes job requirements or prerequisites.
- It's a powerful tool for managing employee performance.
- It helps you guide employee development plans.
- It helps explain the difference between compensation tiers in the same role.

⚡ It covers essential functions and provides compliance with the Americans with Disabilities Act.

⚡ It can protect you from employment discrimination claims.

To hire well, write a job description that's clear on the goals and objectives of the position.

So, how do you do that? And how do you determine the experience, education, and the personality characteristics a good fit would have?

Well, if you are a large corporation you have several meetings and meet with many of the involved people. But let's get real. Most building products leaders are making the decisions on their own or with the help of a key employee or two.

Writing a job description isn't nearly as complicated as you might think.

 There is a downloadable job description form, template and example available in the Hiring Toolkit.

Determine exactly what your business needs.

This is where you can rely on your clarity exercises. Pull from those determinations to help explain what you truly need for the role.

Once you've mapped it out, make sure you review it to see if you're being realistic. Leaders often underestimate OR overestimate the amount of time it will take a new hire to complete the work. If possible, track how long it takes to do the task so you have a reasonable expectation for their performance.

Figure out what goals you have in mind for your new hire.

If you're going to hire and retain a high-potential person, it's extremely important to have clearly defined expectations. I don't simply mean performance expectations. Smart managers know what the person will need to do to hit the performance goals.

HOW TO

SET PERFORMANCE GOALS

Let's say the performance goal is to increase sales by 10%. The current sales level is $1 million. So they are tasked with increasing sales by $100,000 to $1.1 million.

To hit that goal, you need to know several things:

⚡ The average attrition of customers. Can they reasonably expect $1 million in sales from existing clients next year, or do they need to drive more business to make up for lost sales?

⚡ What is the average customer or sale worth?

⚡ On average, how many appointments does it take to get a new sale?

For purposes of this example, let's plan on 10% customer attrition, so they will have $900,000 of existing customer business to count on. To get to $1.1 million, they will need to add $200,000 of sales.

If each sale has a value of $20,000, it will take 55 sales (1,100,000 / $20,000 = 55) to reach goal.

If you know it takes three appointments to get a sale, you know it will take 165 appointments to close $1.1 million of business.

Now you know that your new hire needs to schedule an average of three appointments a week to hit their sales goal. Most managers make the mistake of setting performance goals, but not clarifying the activity needed to realistically achieve those performance goals. This sets up the new hire for failure and the manager for frustration.

By clearly explaining what activities and how many of them they will need to do to hit their goals, you're able to truly set up the new hire for success. Not to mention, it's much easier to quickly identify and address performance issues.

PRO TIP *An easy way to avoid a hiring mistake is by clearly setting and communicating expectations in the interview process. Once you've shared the activity expectations, ask your candidate if they agree your goals are reasonable and achievable. This should spark an engaged conversation if your goals are unreasonable. But if they believe the goals are reasonable, you are both on the same page.*

Decide what skills, experience, and education you require.

This will help you sort through resumes more quickly. If you know that you need someone to be licensed, it's pretty obvious that not having the license will be a deal breaker.

Address the intangibles. What kind of person do you want to be around?

When you take on a new member of your team, it's important to decide in advance if they're the best fit for your company culture. What kind of personality traits and work style will mesh best? (Chances are you've identified what <u>doesn't</u> work well with past hires.) This is where you think about the personality traits and work style of people who are successful in this role and in your company.

Obviously, all this clarity is good for the business, but it is also very desirable to your ideal hires as well.

- ⚡ Great candidates want to know what is expected of them so they can exceed it.

- ⚡ They want to be hired for positions they can excel in now, not something that requires them to work under their skill level for two years.

- ⚡ They want to understand how their role is important and provides value to the organization.

- ⚡ Understanding why and how your role is important is a large part of job security. When people don't know if their position is serving a purpose, they get nervous and start to look around.

If this is the first time you've hired for this role and don't know what is reasonable to expect, include some interview questions that ask experienced candidates about their daily, weekly, and monthly activity in their current role.

section three

ATTRACT
and
RECRUIT

HIRE POWER

HIRE POWER

There are two ways to get great people interested in your openings.

The first one is attraction.

ATTRACTION *Is* MARKETING.

In the attraction stage, we need a lot of eyes on our opportunity to get the few right ones to take action. Many companies post their job ad in one place and hope for the best. This is a high-risk strategy. You are essentially putting all your eggs in one basket.

The second one is recruiting.

RECRUITING *Is* SALES.

In the recruiting stage, we are taking a more targeted approach. We are seeking out people with the experience we want and contacting them about our opportunity. We are moving beyond luck and starting to take control of our hiring process.

Okay, how do we approach hiring with a marketing mindset?

We answer these key questions:

- ⚡ How do we want to be perceived?
- ⚡ Who do we want to get in front of?
- ⚡ Where is our ideal hire at?
- ⚡ What action do we want them to take?

Essentially, it boils down to how and where to show up. This brings me to The Recruiting Plan.

chapter five

The Recruiting **PLAN**

If you're anything like most LBM business owners and managers, your past recruiting plan has consisted of posting your job description and hoping someone good applies. Essentially, you've been rolling the dice and hoping for the best.

If you've done much gambling in your life, you know that relying on luck is a bad plan.

So, let's move beyond luck and get strategic.

You know the saying: failing to plan is planning to fail.

When you decide to get serious about finding and hiring awesome people, you will rely on proven strategies instead of dumb luck.

When you start using a Recruiting Plan instead of a post-and-pray approach to finding qualified people, you start to see that finding qualified people isn't nearly as impossible as you thought it was.

First off, let me explain to you what the Recruiting Plan is **NOT**. It's not a one-size-fits-all checklist that anyone can use to find amazing people for any role. Yes, there are some basic things you can do for almost any opening, but powerful recruiting plans are modified for each opening. They can be as simple as a three-step hiring checklist or as multi-faceted and complicated as you need them to be.

Your Recruiting Plan is essentially the road map that shows you "how" and "where" to show up to find and connect with your ideal hires.

This is why your Recruiting Plan is driven by your **Ideal Hire Profile**.

It can include:
- ⚡ Posting the job
- ⚡ Networking
- ⚡ Sourcing – identifying your keywords
- ⚡ Utilizing long-term talent funnels
- ⚡ Identifying out-of-the-box ideas

The simple reality is, if you get enough qualified candidates by posting the job, you don't need to take it any further. The additional steps are there if you don't have enough qualified candidates from posting the job ad. Considering the shortage of experienced building products professionals, you're going to need to go beyond the basics.

That means you're going to need an Ideal Hire Profile.

Creating Your Ideal Hire Profile

The entire goal of your Recruiting Plan is to get several qualified candidates to choose from. Once you're clear about what you need your new hire to do (remember that job description you created?), you can use the job description to guide you as you develop your Ideal Hire Profile.

So, what's an Ideal Hire Profile?

In marketing this is referred to as customer personas or avatars. It's an idealized version of the person you want to hire. It's the mental image you hold in your mind to help write better job ads, recruiting pitches, and how to decide how and where to show up.

By looking at the job description, you can identify several key characteristics of your ideal hire:

- How much experience do they need in a similar role?
- What kind of personality will work best in the role?
- What software or tools do they need to know how to use?
- Where do they work?
- What do they do in their current job?

Basically, you just need to imagine a person who can hit the ground running and thrive in the role. This is your Ideal Hire Profile.

Your ideal profile doesn't need to be a fancy document; it can be three bullet points or a couple paragraphs. But, I encourage you to actually define it.

PRO TIP Don't fall for the "I'll know it when I see it" line you've told yourself in the past. We're trying to attract them — not just recognize them.

You'll use your ideal hire for almost every aspect of the Recruiting Plan.

Your Ideal Hire Profile will determine:

⚡ How you write your job ad.

⚡ How you sell your organization.

⚡ How you sell the opportunity.

⚡ How you define the ideal hire (they should be able to see themselves in the ad).

⚡ How you craft your recruiting pitches.

⚡ Where you post your job ad:

⚡ Looking for an hourly or manual labor role? Post on Craigslist.

⚡ Looking for a professional-level role? Use Indeed and LinkedIn.

Keeping a mental picture of your dream hire will help you determine how and where to show up in order to attract, connect, and engage the best people.

ATTRACT AND RECRUIT

chapter six

Job Boards
and Job Ads

Big or small, almost every company uses job postings or job ads to let people know about their openings.

It started with hanging a sign in your window, then it moved on to classifieds in the newspaper, then it moved online with big boards like Monster and CareerBuilder. Now, job aggregators like Indeed and ZipRecruiter and social media platforms like LinkedIn and Facebook compete heavily for employer dollars and applicants' attention. Third-party recruiters and large employers use retargeting, AI, and talent mapping to ensure they can find the talent they need. The only certainty around recruiting is that it will constantly be disrupted with a newer, better technology.

There is a reason pretty much everyone who hires uses job ads. They are simple.

Job boards are like a food court at the mall. When you get hungry, you know if you go to the food court you will have a lot of choices. It is the same way with job boards. All the companies put their ads up in the same place, and all the people who want to change jobs know to go there for new job opportunities.

But, as you probably know, simple isn't always easy.

Just because you post a job ad doesn't mean you are going to get the results you want.

It is simple to copy and paste your job description into a job board. **But** *it isn't easy* to get the *right* people interested enough to read your job ad and actually apply.

It is simple to wait for the applicants to roll in after posting your job ad. **But** *it isn't easy* to weed through the dozens of unqualified applicants, looking for the good ones.

It is simple to think, "Well, this is all there is. I have to choose from these three mediocre candidates." So, you hire one and hope for the best. **But** *it isn't easy* to have an underperforming employee who saps your time, energy, and money.

Okay, I think I've made my point … now for the good news.

Posting a job ad is one of the easiest ways you can get new candidates, if you know what to do.

If you can get this right, you will never have to settle again.

I've posted tens of thousands of jobs as a recruiter. I've learned through trial and error how to create a job ad that attracts and engages the right people and "encourages" the wrong people *not* to apply.

The result is a process that will rapidly and dramatically increase your applicant traffic.

❗ WARNING: Your results from job boards and job postings are heavily influenced by environmental factors as well. You will get the best results from job postings on job boards with a lot of traffic or by posting in a larger metro area.

Super Charge Your Job Posting

The biggest mistake people make is using their job description as their job ad. Sure, it's quick and easy to copy and paste your job description into the job posting, but job postings are expensive (especially when you don't get many qualified applicants). At hundreds of dollars per posting, it makes sense to get the most value from your investment by taking the time to craft a compelling job ad that gets results.

 Check out the video on Job Ads in The Hiring Toolkit.

A job description should give a solid overview of the position, set expectations, and legally protect the company. Job descriptions serve an important purpose in the hiring process, but they are usually highly ineffective as job ads (most of them are B-O-R-I-N-G!). Duties, responsibilities, and, by the way, can you lift 20 pounds repeatedly? Wait, what was that? I think I dozed off for a minute.

A JOB DESCRIPTION
is not a
JOB AD.

A well-written job ad is more like marketing copy than a job description. It is based on the job description, but **attracts** the right people **to read it** and **inspires them to apply**.

A well-written job ad includes these key elements:

A Tell and Sell About the Company

Tell them about your company. This is a brief company bio. If you want to work smart, you can probably pull it from your about us page or marketing copy. *An example: XYZ Company was founded in 1978 and serves the residential and commercial construction markets.*

Sell them on it. This is where you share why your company/organization is a great place to work. Include phrases like "we are privately held, offer a family-friendly environment, and foster a culture of success." Brag a little bit. Comments like "We have won numerous awards for our work/work environment" are great details to include (if they're true!).

A Tell and Sell About the Opportunity

Tell them what you are looking for — the "we are seeking" statement. This is where you describe your ideal hire's attributes and experience (e.g., "an outgoing, achievement-oriented sales person"). Share what past successes they should have and what experiences they should demonstrate. Be sure to list any certifications or licenses needed or preferred.

Sell them on the opportunity. What opportunities will the new hire have? What perks will they be eligible for? Include all the great things about working for your company and in this role specifically.

Call-to-Action

In this case, the call-to-action is pretty obvious. We want them to send a resume in. Make sure it is easy for people to apply. Allowing people to applu with social media or online profiles is a great way to increase applications.

PRO TIP *My little soapbox moment:* When you make a prospective hire re-enter all the info on their resume, you will lose a large percentage of the great candidates.

Go through your process and see how long it takes to apply. You need a *very* compelling job if it's more than three minutes. If your process is too arduous, you're much more likely to lose the semi-passive candidate you really want than the active "desperate" candidate. So, if you are telling yourself that you are just weeding out the weak applicants — you are fooling yourself and risk losing great candidates in the process.

PRO TIP *If you're investing in a paid job board like Monster or CareerBuilder, you have the option of including a list of customizable qualifying questions with your job ad. They'll be scored and the results will be sent to you electronically. Always verify any written answer by following up on it during the first interview.*

Now that you've placed your job ad and done some recruiting, it's time to prepare for (hopefully!) all of the applicants who are interested in working for you.

chapter seven

Work
SMARTER

As a building materials dealer, the last thing you likely want to be thinking about and dealing with is hiring. Not only is it likely outside of your comfort zone, it's time-consuming on top of your already full schedule.

I'm going to share some simple ways you can streamline some of the time consuming aspects of hiring. Putting some automated steps in place will enable you to find your right person efficiently, *without* affecting the day-to-day work that needs to be done.

Not sure what that would look like for your business? Don't worry. My simple two-step automation process is so easy, you can set it all up in about five minutes.

Here's how it works:

Step 1: Create an email address for resumes to go to. If you need to, I suggest upgrading to an email provider that will let you use your domain. Resumes@YourCompanyName.com looks a lot better to a candidate than

YourCompanyName@gmail.com. Candidates won't respond to or be that interested in working for someone who doesn't use their domain for their email communication with them.

Step 2: Set up an autoresponder that lets the candidates know what they can expect. This serves the dual purpose of letting them know you got their resume *and* as a rejection letter for the candidates you won't be interviewing.

Here's an example:

Subject: Thank you!

We appreciate your interest in our opening. We will be reviewing resumes within 10 days of their receipt and will be contacting qualified candidates to arrange the next step in the process. If you don't hear from us within 14 days of your submittal, please assume that we are pursuing candidates who fit our needs more closely.

We appreciate your interest in our company. You can learn more at (insert link to website or if there is a hiring specific area — link to that).

Have a great day!

Signature

*This email box is not monitored, so please don't reply to this message to check the status of your application.

There is a pdf version of this template in the Hiring Toolkit.

See how easy that was?

Now you have all your applications safely in one location. Each applicant knows their resume has been received, and there's no need to draft a formal rejection letter. *Boom!*

PRO TIP *If you are doing a lot of hiring, you may want to invest in a formal applicant tracking system. But, these two tips can turn your email client into an effective tracking tool. In fact, I used this system for the first five years I was a recruiter!*

Review a Resume in 10 Seconds

The next step to streamlining your process is a quick first-round resume sort. I know what you're probably thinking. "What?! How could someone possibly thoroughly review a resume in 10 seconds?"

Well, for starters, I didn't say *thoroughly*.

The 10-second resume review is how I determine which candidates are worth a more in-depth look.

Look for
ONE REASON
they won't work.

It comes down to one rule: I'm looking for reasons they won't work.

Depending on your market and the appeal of your job, you could get hundreds of responses to your ad. While this might seem awesome at first, it creates an overwhelming time-suck.

To put it in perspective: if you spent one minute per resume and you have 500 responses, you will spend 8.33 hours reviewing resumes. That's a full work day and then some.

Now, some of you are struggling to get 15 responses, but once you implement my process, you will be happy you set up some automation processes — I promise.

Here's a quick tutorial on rapid-fire resume scanning, so you can focus the bulk of your time on talking to the right candidates.

Check location first: Do they live in the right area? Is it a reasonable commute? I keep Google maps open so I can easily plug in the town name if I'm not familiar with it.

Read over their titles: Are the titles in line with the position I'm looking for? If I'm looking for a Territory Sales Rep and they've been a Sales Manager for the past five years, I will likely move on — unless it's clear by their resume that they don't have direct reports. Titles and responsibilities vary greatly from company to company. Be sure to verify your assumption by quickly scanning their achievements in the position. If they've shared very little information on their resume, ask them for clarification before you reject them out of hand.

Check their channels or customer base: Is their experience in the right channel? With the right client base? Do I think there is enough similarity for them to be able to get up to speed quickly?

Skip down to read successes: Is their resume basically a copy and paste from their job description? Or is it full of quantifiable examples of their success? I want to know someone knows their numbers and can prove their successes — especially if they're heading for a sales position.

Is their resume visually appealing? It might sound a bit snobby, but your resume is supposed to be a written example of you putting "your best foot forward." If it's a mess or disorganized, I tend to assume that the candidate won't be too concerned with the quality of work they do for me.

You might be wondering: what about their objective or summary? Frankly, I don't care about that part of the resume at all at this point. I use the objective more often *to rule people out than in.*

Many people forget to adjust their objective, or list the wrong company name or title. This doesn't indicate a strong attention to detail or strong interest in the position to me. The summary is often too wordy — I am not going to read a paragraph before I know if you have the right experience.

Obviously, this is the 30,000-foot view of the resume. Once I've narrowed it down to the 10% to 20% of applicants who fit the criteria, I examine their credentials closely before I contact them. Frankly, I prefer to spend my time talking to people who have a more than reasonable chance of being a fit.

RYG: A Simple System that Changes Everything

Chances are you've correctly navigated a stoplight recently. That means you've got the basic concept of red, yellow, and green nailed. (If not … well, this tip will be a useful tool for you in two ways!)

Did you know: you can use the same method to quickly review and rank candidates?

Yep. It's all part of a handy little system called RYG.

Why RYG? Why, Red, Yellow, Green, of course!

Green (YES!) – You want to reach out to them ASAP.

Yellow (Caution) – Hmm … they have good and bad aspects.

Red (STOP) – For some reason they aren't a fit.

As you're going through responses to your job ad, add a label or change the subject line of the email to include the color ranking next to the candidate's name. This allows you to sort your responses and focus on the "green" candidates first.

The goal is to free you up to focus on the prospective hires who are the closest to your ideal.

Hopefully, there will be enough "green" candidates that you can invite them to interview and choose your best candidate from the mix.

But, unfortunately, that doesn't always happen. Because of that potential gap, it's good to have your list of "yellow" candidates on hand to see if anyone else is worth interviewing.

INSIDER INFO

NOT GETTING ENOUGH RESPONSES FROM YOUR JOB AD?

Do these three things:

1. **Make sure you're selling the opportunity.**

   Review your job ad and answer these questions:

   ⚡ Did you basically copy and paste your job description? If so, be sure to transform it into a job ad.

   ⚡ Have you written it with "What's in it for me?" from the candidate's perspective?

   ⚡ Can a candidate look at it and say, "Oh, I can see a career here!" Or do they simply see a job?

2. **Make sure that your ad is getting in front of the right people.**

   If you are looking for a professional employee, try LinkedIn. If you are looking for an hourly position, try Craigslist. Need industry experience? Try local associations and groups.

   Need a recent college grad? Connect with Career Services and professors.

   I've had good luck with Indeed.com for all sorts of positions. Use the pay-per-click option and you can get applicants for a very reasonable cost.

3. Post it in multiple places.

Personally, I like getting in front of a wide variety of audiences because you never know where the right person is coming from. When I am working on a search, **I use at least 12 sources to find candidates**. If you are only using one medium to attract and find candidates, you are missing out on a huge number of potential candidates.

Now, job postings can be expensive, so I'm not advocating spending hundreds of dollars on 12 postings. Utilize free and low-cost platforms to share your opportunity with your ideal hires.

chapter eight

Sourcing: *Finding* Your Ideal Hires

When you come to the realization the job postings just aren't cutting it, you still have lots of options to find qualified people. I'm going to start with the easiest one. This is the first step to go beyond hoping people apply to your openings and making your own luck.

Sourcing means proactively seeking out people who have the experience you want. Learning how to source means you're taking control back. You aren't going to wait for the stars to align or for a genie to appear; you're going to take control of your destiny and change your business and your life, one hire at a time.

The best part ... it's so easy when you know what to do.

You can source (find) resumes and profiles **for free** from a variety of online sources like Indeed.com, Craigslist, LinkedIn, Facebook, and Google. If you have a budget for recruiting, you can pay for access to the resume databases on job boards like Monster, Dice, or CareerBuilder.

I have used almost every sourcing tool available and have found that some are better for different types of jobs than others. Overall, Indeed and LinkedIn deliver tremendous results for free or very minimal costs. I'd suggest you start with one of them.

A couple of points before you start your sourcing adventure:

⚡ The people you will identify haven't expressed interest in your role or organization, so you will need to "sell" the opportunity a bit more than to someone who applied directly to your postings.

⚡ To get the best results from your list, be prepared to contact them more than once and through different mediums.

⚡ Don't expect to hear back from everyone. Sometimes an email goes to an account they might not check very often. I often get delayed responses from people I reached out to about a search months earlier. Shoot for a 20% or higher response rate from your sourcing efforts.

⚡ Realize that targeted sourcing is meant to provide the best matches, not the most matches. If you can get three qualified people interested for an interview, that's probably enough. All you need in the end is one.

⚡ This is definitely more work than "posting and praying" but when executed well, it's infinitely more powerful.

Where can you source online?

You have a wide variety of options when it comes to sourcing candidates online. It will largely be dictated by your budget.

Free Options:

⚡ LinkedIn — The larger your network (1st connections) is the more value you can get from a free LinkedIn Account. LinkedIn frequently changes what you can do with a free account, and their goal is to get you to upgrade.

⚡ Indeed — You'll need to create a free employer account to access the resumes to see if there is anyone you are interested in. If you want to contact them you will need to buy a subscription for contacts.

⚡ Craigslist (best for hourly, trade, or manual positions)

⚡ Associations/Groups/Certification Programs — They often list their members on their website and you can review them and look the people up using Google or LinkedIn to find more information on them.

Paid Options:

⚡ Big Boards: Monster, CareerBuilder, Dice, etc.

⚡ Job Aggregators: Indeed, Simply Hired, ZipRecruiter

⚡ LinkedIn: upgraded plans with InMails, etc.

⚡ Some Associations/Groups/Certification Programs

⚡ Local or Niche Job Boards and Resume Databases

Your online resources are going to change and evolve constantly. Simply Googling "resume databases" will give you some ideas.

HOW TO

FIGURE OUT YOUR KEYWORDS

Before you can even start sourcing, you need to figure out your keywords. That's where the 5W's come in. They are a great way to build the framework of your search strings. Don't worry, there'll be more on search strings in the Boolean Search section coming up. For now, just grab a notebook and start answering the following questions. The more keywords you have to work with, the better your search will go.

These are some of the question you will ask yourself.

Please note: *Not all of these questions will apply to every position. But, it's a good practice to work through these questions to be sure you're looking in the right places.*

Who:
- ⚡ Who does your ideal hire currently work for?
- ⚡ Who are your ideal hire's customers?
- ⚡ Who are the vendors or suppliers they would work with regularly?

What:
- ⚡ What job titles do similar positions have?
- ⚡ What certifications do they have?
- ⚡ What industry associations do they belong to?
- ⚡ What trade journals or magazines do they read?

⚡ What trade shows or conventions do they attend?

⚡ What are keywords or industry jargon they have on their resume or profile?

Where:

⚡ Where do they work?

⚡ Where are they located?

⚡ Where can they do this job from? (Can it be virtual?)

When:

⚡ When do they need to do this work? (Does it have to be 9-5?)

⚡ When do I need them to start?

⚡ When will the need for this position end or this project wrap up?

Why:

⚡ Why does this position need to be filled?

⚡ Why would someone want this job?

By using the 5W's, you create a blueprint for the type of person you're looking for. This is a simple way to clarify and be able to share the "I'll know it when I see it" aspect of hiring. This will help you and your HR team to write better job ads and identify the best applicants when they apply. It will help in more ways than just finding keywords to use when sourcing if you are strategic.

PRO TIP *As you work through your Recruiting Plan, you may see things on people's resumes or profiles that inspire you to look in a different direction. For example, I often learn about relevant associations by noticing what candidates have listed on their resume. Then I can check out the association to see if it would be a good place for me to look for people. I would encourage you to follow your instincts on this, but always remember to circle back to your Ideal Hire Profile to be sure you're still looking for what you need and haven't gotten completely off track.*

HOW TO

USE BOOLEAN OPERATORS

You may only vaguely recall "Boolean Search" from your days in the library, but this powerful tool will become crucial to your recruiting success. Boolean Search Strings allow you to search a huge database of potentials and narrow it down to the ones that are most likely to meet your requirements. Boolean operators such as AND, OR, NOT, and NEAR allow you to limit, widen, or define your search.

By combining the information from your Recruiting Plan with basic Boolean logic, you can drill down through the millions of people on LinkedIn to the 40 to 50 who have the experience you want and are within a commutable distance.

Below are some of the common operators used.

AND: the search results must include all keywords linked by AND.

OR: the results will include responses with any of the keywords.

"": by placing multiple words in quotation marks, the search engine will see it as one word and only return results that match the term in quotes exactly.

(): by placing multiple keywords in parentheses, you can "group" terms together and the search engine will read the operators between each set of parentheses and use those results to compare against the other set.

Interested in digging deeper into Boolean? Check out www.booleanblackbelt.com.

Here's an example of how to use Boolean search string for an outside LBM sales person:

Industry or overall product category + job title
Lumberyard AND Sales

Specific Product Names or Types + Job Title
(Lumber OR Sliding OR Doors OR Roofing) AND Sales

Competitors + Job Title
("ABC Supply" OR "84 Lumber" OR "US LBM") AND Sales

You can see how the keywords you developed in the 5W's exercise can turn into a powerful search string. Just be warned, these are general rules and will often work but it's always best to check the support docs for the best practices for the site you're searching.

chapter nine

Recruiting:
Connecting with
the Right People

So, you've networked and mastered the art of Boolean. You have a big, digital "stack" of online profiles of people who appear to have what your company needs, putting you *way* ahead of most of your competitors.

Feels great, right?

Now all you have to do is turn that pile of potential into actual interest.

"What? Talk to someone about a job who hasn't applied for it? That would be so AWKWARD! No, thanks…"

Alright, alright. So maybe it's not *quite* as simple as I made it sound.

If the thought of picking up the phone and asking someone if they want to work for you makes you queasy, here's some good news: the Internet, along with social media, has changed the recruiting game dramatically.

Now, instead of picking up the phone, it's just a matter of hitting send on a well-crafted email.

For those of us looking for talent, the Internet's been a game changer for finding "our" people. Because you're able to take a sneak peek at someone's background *before* initiating the conversation, there's no more flying blind. All you have to do is approach candidates with a highly targeted message that resonates with them. And, for those you skip because their backgrounds don't entirely suit you, they're none the wiser.

Phew.

"Oh, but the good ones already have jobs. If I reach out to them about my opportunity, they may get offended ... or think I'm sleazy."

Welcome to one of the largest misconceptions people have about recruiting. **The vast majority of people you will contact about an opportunity will be flattered that you reached out to them.** They may not be interested in making a change, but if you're personable and professional, you will rarely offend anybody.

I've often said that recruiting belongs under "Sales and Marketing" in the company organization chart. Recruiting was misfiled under HR years ago, and it's been trying to escape ever since.

Attraction is marketing.

Recruiting is sales.

Hiring is closing the deal.

"If I'm going to **play,** I prefer to **WIN.**"

As I've stated before: if I'm going to play a game, I prefer to win. I assume you feel the same way, so let me help you. Recruiting is as complex and strategic as a game of chess. Like any great chess player will tell you, to come out on top, you first need to master the basics.

Before you kick off your recruiting journey, make sure you've got a firm grasp on the foundational principles.

Connecting is the heart of recruiting.

While it's easy to assume the only connecting that matters here is with "the right person," to be successful as a recruiter, you need to make a lot of connections. Period.

If you only contact three or four potential hires, the chances you'll find and hire the rockstar employee of your dreams are pretty hopeless. On the other hand, if your job ad is visible to thousands of people, but your message isn't compelling enough for anyone to connect with, your results will be just as abysmal. You need to connect with enough people to find "the one," and craft a captivating message that connects their goals and aspirations to your opportunity.

When you're marketing intelligently, you're focused on getting your message in front of the people most likely to buy your product or service. If you're a taxi service that caters to people who can't drive, you're unlikely to invest in Sirius/XM ad campaigns. You're more likely to spend your marketing dollars on mediums your target customer uses every day, like public transit.

Proactive recruiting follows a similar train of thought. We focus our recruiting efforts and dollars on the places we're most likely to find our target candidate. While it's impossible to predict where the best person will come from, you should certainly have some good ideas based on past hires or market knowledge. If you're new to proactive recruiting, you'll need to try out a variety of sources before determining where your "sweet spots" are.

In the end, it all comes down to positioning your opportunity in a manner that will appeal to your target audience. In this case, your target audience is people who fit your Ideal Hire Profile.

REMINDER: The **Ideal Hire Profile** is the heart of your recruiting strategy. To find the right person for the position, you need to create a clear profile of your ideal hire in terms of education, experience, and, of course, personality. Once you've got that in place, we know *where to go* and *how to show up* to attract their attention and get them interested in our opportunity.

The more you can compel and excite people to action, the better your responses will be. By applying your marketing know-how to recruiting, you'll ensure you make enough connections to find "the one."

Now you've found the people who fit your needs, it's time to start connecting with them on a deeper level. Just as the best sales occur when someone *buys* something versus being *sold* something, the best hires happen when the recruit "buys in" to your vision and wants to be part of it.

You can be the best marketer in the world, but if you can't connect with people and close the deal, you won't win at hiring. Until they accept your job offer, nothing's been "sold." You must be able to transition from marketing to selling your opportunity.

HOW TO

NETWORK LIKE A RECRUITER

Not everyone enjoys networking. But if you're looking to grow your team or your business, you have to learn to embrace networking.

I happen to love networking. I love meeting new people, making connections, and learning about the latest and greatest things. But, I realize that to many people, networking can be something they dread. (I happen to be married to one of those people.)

I truly believe that networking is a skill anyone can master.

Learning how to start and move the conversation along with talented people can truly be a game-changer for non-recruiters, plus it's much, much easier than most people think.

A bit introverted? No worries, this approach works for even the most reserved people. Everyone in business can benefit from networking, *especially* if you are trying to hire.

Set Your Intention. As with most things in life, your attitude determines your results. If you think "poaching" employees is evil, you won't have any success. When you head out to a networking event, go with the intention to connect people. Connecting people and learning how you can provide value to them is the number one way to build your social capital.

Create Real Connections. Don't try to talk to everyone. If you have identified key people you want to talk with, seek them out. Otherwise, mingle intentionally, seeking people with whom you can create a genuine connection.

Be Curious. Curiosity is the key. By simply asking questions and listening to the answers, you will learn everything you need to know.

Use Strategic Small Talk. This is the key to undercover recruiting. By asking simple and common questions, we can learn everything we need to know about a potential hire. You will find better hires, make better connections, and learn more (and likely have more fun) if you spend networking events asking questions and listening to the answers.

 How To Network Like a Recruiter video training and PDF are available in the Hiring Toolkit.

CURIOUSITY and STRATEGIC SMALL TALK are the keys to success networking.

chapter ten

The Recruiting Pitch

"So, do you want to come work for me?"

How in the world do you start this conversation?

Answer: with a kick-ass Recruiting Pitch, of course!

Your Recruiting Pitch's sole purpose is to get your target candidate to talk with you.

Use the WII-FM (What's In It For Me) technique to "get in their head" so you better know how to answer: What about this job would appeal to them? How would they benefit? Why should they bother to respond to you?

Developing your Recruiting Pitch should be fun and exciting, so if you're feeling a bit sluggish, grab a cup of coffee or do a few jumping jacks before you start. Energy and enthusiasm go a long way.

Your Recruiting Pitch should be fluid. It can be adapted for face-to-face communications, emails, social media posts, and direct messages. Your Recruiting Pitch also can be used by others to help you. For example, family and friends, a powerful networking tool, can forward it to people who might be a fit. Or perhaps you have an applicant who is not right for the role but knows a friend who might be. Remember: You never know what unlikely source is going to hand you the referral of your dreams.

PRO TIP *Don't start from scratch every time. You can create a template for your job ads, Recruiting Pitches, and other recruiting communications, and fill in the position-specific details. Just be sure to read it closely and make sure it's all still accurate and relevant.*

Fortunately, if you've been doing the exercises in this book, you've already developed most of the aspects of your Recruiting Pitch. Now we just need to pull them together.

Rock Your Recruiting Pitch

A great Recruiting Pitch is ...

⚡ Personalized

⚡ Engaging

⚡ Fluid and adapted to the situation

⚡ Accurate. Don't over promise and under deliver.

A great Recruiting Pitch usually includes ...

Company info:

⚡ Basic company information

⚡ Anything "cool" about your product, company, or you

⚡ Your website and any other relevant information so the candidate can easily research you and the company.

Details about the position:

⚡ Highlights pulled from your Ideal Hire Profile

⚡ The job ad or a link to it

⚡ A concise, yet compelling, blurb about the opportunity.

Personalized information:

⚡ Why you thought they'd be a good fit, or be interested

⚡ An acknowledgment of their achievements, or similar ego stroke.

A Call-to-Action:

⚡ An easy way for them to apply or to continue the conversation

⚡ An alternative close; asking for a referral.

WARNING: Don't let efficiency overrule etiquette. Just like a photocopied thank you note, you lose a lot of the value when it's clear little to no thought was put into your pitch or that it's obviously a template.

Your sourcing efforts will produce a variety of people: active job seekers, referral sources, and candidates you're trying to recruit from their current job. Each of these requires a slightly different approach. Sending the same email template to all of them won't just irritate people, it'll also result in a very low response rate.

Spend the extra time to make sure they're getting a message that's appropriate for them. Of course, you can create a template for active job seekers and referral sources, but when it comes to direct recruits, you're going to want to personalize the message as much as possible. They will require a bit more ego stroking than an active job seeker.

Examples of Recruiting Pitches

Now that you've got your game face on and understand the basic elements of a Recruiting Pitch, let's get specific, shall we?

Included here are several templates and sample scripts. You're welcome to use these templates verbatim (just be sure to fill in the sections in parentheses), but I would encourage you to wordsmith them a bit and make them your own. You want your Recruiting Pitch to be an accurate representation of who you are. If my language sounds nothing like yours, simply use these as a guide to create your own custom templates.

The Good

Here's a very basic example of a Recruiting Pitch email that's effective, but not very personalized. It's good to use something like this when you're reaching out to many people about an opportunity. By being vague, it frees you up to reach out to anyone who would be an active or passive candidate online.

Subject: Career Opportunity with (company name)

Hi (first name),

My name is (first name); I am the (your job title) for (company name). I found your information online and wanted to reach out to you about an opportunity we have available. Based on your background, it seems like you could be a good fit.

Here's a link to learn more about our company (Company Web Page).

And a brief overview of the opportunity:

Insert job ad or link to job ad here

If this seems like it could be a good fit for you, please apply online or simply reply to this email with a current resume so we can continue the conversation.

If this isn't the right fit for you, please feel free to pass it on to anyone you think would be qualified and interested. Also, feel free to let me know if there are any other types of opportunities with our organization that would interest you. I look forward to connecting with you!

Thanks for your time and interest!

Signature… (Be sure to include your email address and potentially your phone number)

Things to note about this message:

- ⚡ I explain how I found them. Otherwise they may assume your email is spam.
- ⚡ They get an ego stroke.
- ⚡ They're invited to check out the business for themselves. I give them the website so they can learn more about the company, as well as the job ad.
- ⚡ I ask them to follow up if they're interested.
- ⚡ If they aren't interested, I invite them to pass this info on to someone who might be a fit.
- ⚡ I thank them for their time. Courtesy goes a long way in inspiring referrals.
- ⚡ The email offers multiple ways to get in touch.

The Better

By contrast, here's an improved Recruiting Pitch email. You'll notice it's a bit more energetic and upbeat. It also includes more information for the candidate, eliminating the need for them to click a link or visit a website. You would use a template like this for a candidate who has a good background, but isn't a highly targeted direct recruit.

Subject: Connecting about a career opportunity in (your industry)

Hi (first name),

My name is (first name); I am the (your job title) for (company name). We're an award-winning, family-owned lumberyard that is growing fast. We're looking for some great outside sales people to help us continue to grow! I found your profile online, and based on your sales successes, it seems like you might be a great fit for our team. I'd love to connect with you and learn more about what you're looking for in the next step of your career.

I realize that you may want to know a bit more about us, so here's a link to our website as well (Company Web Page). If you want to learn more about the product line(s) you'd be selling, you can check them out here. (hyperlink to products page).

As far as the opportunity, right now we're seeking results-oriented sales people who have experience calling on builders and contractors.

For more information about our openings, go here: (link to job ad)

If you'd be interested in talking further, simply reply to this email or apply online to the opportunity that interests you. Don't worry. We will respect your confidentiality. No one will know you're talking with us.

If this isn't the right fit for you, please feel free to pass it on to anyone you think would be qualified and interested. Also, feel free to let me know if there are any other types of opportunities with our organization that would interest you. I look forward to connecting with you soon!

Thanks for your time and interest.

Signature… (Be sure to include an email address — and if you want — a phone number.)

Things to note about this message:

⚡ The language is upbeat and positive.

⚡ Existing success of your company is implied, and the candidate is being invited "to help us continue to grow."

⚡ The candidate's success is also mentioned. (Again with the ego stroke.)

⚡ It's geared towards opportunities, and the next steps in their career, versus their next job.

⚡ Easy access to information is provided. That shows the company is an "open book."

⚡ It has a very brief overview of hireable attributes before the link to the job ad.

⚡ Confidentiality is addressed. Ideally, you're always respecting people's confidentiality, but actually saying you will in writing puts a lot of people's minds at ease.

⚡ Includes an alternative close: asking for a referral.

⚡ You've thanked the candidate for his or her time. Gratitude is always a great practice.

The Best

For this pitch to be as effective as possible, it must be highly personalized. Use this template when you're reaching out to your competitor's top sales person, or some other dream candidate who's currently playing for the competition. To improve your chances of landing "the big one," you need to spend time researching and crafting your message.

"Oh, I can skip this part. I won't be recruiting from my competitors."

Silly rabbit. Unless you have a handshake agreement or you know they are intense about enforcing their non-compete, or if you do business with them, this is where the game really gets interesting. It's also where you will leave the vast majority of your competition behind.

There's a ton you can learn from communicating with your competitor's employees. Employees, particularly if they're frustrated, will tell you all about their compensation plan, their benefits package, and many other things you'd love to know about your competition.

Not only should you strive to have the best possible people on your team, this process is one of the best ways to find out what you're up against as far as recruiting talent goes.

By skipping this step, you're letting fear or discomfort hinder your company's potential. Get over it. Until you start talking to them, you won't know what is or isn't possible. Remember, there's nothing wrong with having a conversation.

An example:

Subject: Impressive!

Hi (first name),

My name is (your name); I am the (your title) at (company). I wanted to reach out to congratulate you on your success (ideally, this is a specific success). I was impressed!

Based on what I've learned about you, I think you could be a good fit for our team. I'd love to learn what you'd be looking for in the next step of your career.

If you're open to a confidential conversation, I'd be happy to schedule a call, a lunch, or we could just meet for coffee.

If you aren't ready to have a conversation yet — just take this as a compliment and know that you're making an impression.

If you want to set something up, feel free to reply to this email or just give me a call at (#).

Signature – include email address and phone number(s)

Things to notice about this message:

⚡ Their achievement is the focus.

⚡ It gives them reasons why you think they'd be a good fit for your organization.

⚡ The tone is direct, yet low-key.

⚡ Offers several options for connecting: phone, in person, lunch, or coffee.

⚡ Gives them an easy out, which also makes you look like "a good guy." It also increases the likelihood of getting a response just letting you know that now isn't the right time for them to make a change.

⚡ Addresses confidentiality concerns, and gives them many easy ways to contact you.

⚡ It doesn't rush them. This is the kind of email people keep around for months. The day their boss irritates them is when they dig it out and send you a message.

. . . .

PRO TIP *Be flexible. You will want to work harder to connect with your targeted recruits. If they want to meet for coffee at 8 p.m. on a Tuesday, figure out how to make it work. They will be highly concerned about keeping the meeting discrete. In my experience, meeting for coffee is the number one choice of passive candidates. It's a level playing field, and can be over in 20 minutes if it goes poorly.*

. . . .

❶ WARNING: Don't treat the first meeting like an interview. It's a conversation. If you launch into your canned interview questions, you will lose them. This is a conversation that will dictate if there will be interviews. You're selling yourself and your company to them.

Asking for Referrals

On your recruiting journey, you inevitably came up with people who would be good referral sources. Learning to ask effectively for referrals can open doors to people you may not be able to find on your own. Here's a sample of how to ask (a stranger) for a referral:

Subject: Networking

Hi (first name),

My name is (your name); I am a (your job title) with (company). I found your information online and wanted to reach out to you. Your background in (area of expertise) is very impressive. We are in the process of hiring a (insert job title). I realize this role is beneath your level of experience, but I wanted to reach out to you to see if you know of anyone who might be less established in their career for whom this would be a good opportunity.

Here is some additional information on the opportunity (include job ad). The compensation for this position will depend on experience, but will likely be between $40,000 - $50,000.

Thanks so much for your time and assistance. If there is ever anything I can do to assist you, please just let me know!

Signature

Things to note about this message:

⚡ Their achievements are recognized right off the bat.

⚡ It includes the compensation range for your role, if possible. People are more likely to pass on an opportunity if it includes some "meatier" details.

⚡ The message is easy for them to forward or share.

⚡ You stress your gratitude, as you thank them for their time and assistance.

The Follow-Up

To get the best results, **you must be willing to reach out to people more than once**.

Don't assume that once you've sent one email, your job is done. You'll need to reach out to people several times through different mediums to truly position yourself for success.

Your level of effort and follow up should directly correlate to your level of interest in the candidate. If your interest level is low, leave it at one email. If your interest is high, be prepared to make a greater effort.

An example:

Subject: Follow up to first email about (job title) at (company name)

Hi (first name),

My name is (your name); I am a (job title) with (company). I reached out to you a few days ago about an opportunity with our company. I wanted to reach out to you again to see if this is something you might be interested in. If it isn't, just let me know so I can take you off my list.

We are looking for a (open job title) in (location). Here is some more information. (insert job ad)

Thanks so much for your time! If this doesn't seem like a good fit for you, but you'd be interested in other roles within our organization, please let me know. Otherwise, feel free to pass this on to anyone you feel would be interested in a role such as this.

Signature

Things to notice about this message:

⚡ You identify yourself clearly. It gives your name and the company name.

⚡ It's a gentle reminder that this isn't the first contact.

⚡ The tone is neutral; it doesn't shame or blame them for not responding.

⚡ It gives them a way to "opt out" by inviting them to let you know if they aren't interested.

⚡ This email can easily be adapted for a third (and final) touch email.

The Bottom Line

It's a great time to be on the hunt for new team members. Thanks to the internet and social media, learning about and connecting with potential hires has never been easier. So, take advantage of it. Don't be shy. Perfect your Recruiting Pitch and reach out to those ideal hires, whatever their state of employment may be.

Always approach any new connection with high energy and enthusiasm, and remember to tailor any pitch to the individual you're speaking to. You'll be surprised how well solid knowledge of a prospective hire's background can go over in an initial dialogue. Be personable, respectful, and, above all, have the courage to get in touch with people you may be hesitant to contact. Remember, there's nothing wrong with simply having a conversation. You never know what might manifest if you just *ask*.

If you get stuck or feel like you're just not sure what to say, feel free to use the templates and examples in this chapter as your inspiration. They're here to help.

PRO TIP *When you're sourcing, you'll often come across great candidates for positions you aren't actively looking for. You may be searching for a bookkeeper and come across a stellar salesperson with industry experience. Depending on the candidate's background, you may want to just hold on to their resume until you're ready to hire for that position or you may want to start the conversation right now.*

INSIDER INFO

SMILING AND DIALING

Sometimes an email just isn't enough. For candidates you're really interested in, take the time to pick up the phone and call them.

You won't always have a phone number available, but if you do, it's worth the effort. I'm not a huge advocate of scripts for phone conversations; I prefer to have an outline on hand that reminds me of the points I want to make. However, I am a "talker" and I have made thousands of these calls. Use a script if it helps you feel confident. Again, be sure to practice the script out loud before you make your first call.

The Good – Voicemail Script

"Hi, this message is for (first name). My name is (first name); I am the (your job title) at (company). I found your information online and wanted to reach out to you about an (open job title) opening we have in (location) right now. Based on your background, it seems like it could be a great fit. I'd love to chat with you to see if it is something that may be of interest to you. You can reach me at (phone number). That number again is (phone number). I will also send an email with some additional info — you can get back to me that way as well. Thanks, and have a great day!"

Things to notice about this message:

⚡ It says who the message is for. Seems simple, but many messages never get delivered because the daughter took over dad's cell phone and deletes this message because, clearly, it isn't for her.

⚡ The language is direct and to the point in a friendly, engaging manner.

⚡ You give them the phone number twice. People are rarely ready with a pen for your number. If you give it twice, they're likely to have the pen in hand by the time you repeat it.

⚡ It mentions an email. Using two methods to follow up with people almost guarantees they will get the message.

⚡ The voicemail ends on an upbeat and friendly tone.

⚡ Remember: Talk slowly and enunciate clearly.

The Better – Voicemail Script

This script is ideal for moments when you have a specific reason for reaching out to someone. It's also intentionally vague. Sometimes, it's easier to go into a Recruiting Pitch when you have a live person to talk to.

Hi (first name), my name is (your name). I am the (your job title) at (company). I just wanted to reach out to you and congratulate you on (whatever achievement or award you're aware of). I saw it in the paper and wanted to connect with you. I'd love to chat if you have a few minutes. You can give me a call at (number). Congratulations again, and I look forward to connecting with you. Again, this is (your name) and the number is (number).

The Best – A Live Conversation

Email has made it much easier to start the dialogue, but true connections are made through conversations. Just make sure you have practiced your Recruiting Pitch and are ready for any questions the candidate may have. I promise, you will be pleasantly surprised at how easy these conversations can be.

section four

INTERVIEWS
and
OFFERS

HIRE POWER

Wahoo! You've found all these great candidates and are ready to interview the best ones!

Now, how do you know which one is "the one"?

With a kick-ass selection process, of course. The selection process includes all interviews, pre-employment testing or assessments, reference checks, and any other steps you take to make sure you're hiring the right person **before** you give them an offer.

There is no "one size fits all" selection process. They vary greatly from company to company, job to job. What's needed to qualify and select a fast food counter worker won't be sufficient for selecting your sales manager.

But, I do have a selection process that can work well for any position if you adapt it to fit.

chapter eleven

Interview
like a **PRO**

Interviewing is a key part of making the best hire for your business. The thing to remember is that interviewing requires more effort than just asking a few standard questions.

With the right process and tools, interviewing will help you weed out those who won't work, as well as help you find the one who does.

Here's the selection process I recommend:

Step 1. Talk about the deal breakers.

Is there anything less-than-ideal about the position you're hiring for? Working weekends, a questionable neighborhood, far from public transportation? If so, be sure to disclose this in the first few emails. Similarly, what are your deal breakers? Do you require that your hire have a college degree, reliable transportation, or a specific certification? I'm sure you've included that information in your job description, but it doesn't hurt to remind candidates in your initial emails. Just this one step will save you (and your candidates) so much time.

Step 2. Use phone interviews.

Even if they're local. Really! It will save you time and offer insight into their general demeanor and how they come across on the phone — particularly important if they'll be working in a sales or public-facing role. A phone interview is the perfect time to ask **functional questions** — those questions that determine if a job applicant can do the job you are hiring for. That way, when you get to the face-to-face interviews, you know you're dealing with people who can handle the basics of the job. You can then focus your interviewing efforts on behavioral-based interview questions and how well they will fit in at your organization.

Step 3. Conduct face-to-face interviews. In person or on video.

Now it's getting serious. We like the candidate enough to invite them back for a more detailed conversation. This is often the first time they will see your face or your office, so make sure you're prepared. Face-to-face interviews are where we start to dig in to see if they are going to be able to do the job and fit in. This is where **behavioral and situational interviews** come into play.

Step 4: Use your selection tools.

Once you've narrowed it down to your final candidates, this is the time to use pre-hire projects to make sure they can do the work. Use pre-employment assessments to make sure you're setting them (and yourself) up for success.

Step 5: Extend the offer.

This is (usually) the fun part. As you're moving your candidate through the interview process, make sure you're talking about compensation as you go. Also, make sure that your candidates know about any other forms they might be asked to sign: non-competes, non-disclosure agreements, drugs tests, etc.

HOW TO

LOOK FOR
CONTRARY EVIDENCE

It's common knowledge that most interviewers make up their minds about candidates in the first few minutes of the interview.

Typically, the process starts by reviewing their resume, obviously; you see something you like, so you set up the interview.

When you start talking to them, you like them. You really, really like them!

From that moment on, all you do is look for evidence that proves you're right for liking that candidate. You look for evidence to prove that they're a great fit for your team and for your position. You kind of gloss over the things they say — even those that should be a cause of concern for you — simply because everything else just feels so good.

Now, unfortunately, you tend to like everyone, and that hasn't turned out so well when you've interviewed in the past.

So, what does contrary evidence have to do with all this?

When you find yourself falling in love with the candidate and everything seems to be great, just — STOP. Mentally stop and readjust your mindset. Start asking more questions and **dig deep**.

When you keep saying, "Oh, I love them, they're perfect," stop and evaluate what they're saying, not what you're feeling about them.

It's a little bit tricky because you've got to catch yourself.

You need to pay attention to what you're thinking. Stop in your tracks and assess the person. Stop continuing to prove that you are right to think they're a great fit.

This is equally true for when you've decided, "Nope, they're not a fit. They're too green for the job." Instead of proving to yourself that you're right, flip your script in your mind. Start thinking: "What can a green person bring to this position? Is there something I am missing here? Okay, they're fresh; I can train them in my way."

Searching for contrary evidence can give you a more thorough review of the candidate and their potential with your company.

You don't want to start moving toward an answer and keep validating yourself. It's pointless, and it's a waste of time. If you're going to spend 20 minutes on an interview anyway, you might as well make sure that you're making the right hire and not just confirming that you were right all along. It's better to realize you are wrong in the interview than after they've been working for you for two weeks.

Using contrary evidence during the interviewing process is a powerful trick that could mean the difference between a hiring mistake and a hiring win. It takes time to practice, but it's worth it.

chapter twelve

Phone Interviews:
The Best Kept Secret

Phone interviews are awesome for many reasons, but the most tangible one is the fact that they will save you a TON of time. No matter where you are — no matter how small of a town you're in — it will take at least 10 to 15 minutes for somebody to get in their car, drive to your office, get out, wait in the waiting room, and then sit down to get interviewed. Common courtesy dictates that the interview should be a bit longer than it took the interviewee to get to you. That means each interview should last for at least 15 minutes.

So, what do you do if you realize relatively quickly that this isn't going to be a fit (say five minutes into the interview)? If you want to avoid offending your interviewee, you'll be stuck trying to make the interview last for 15 to 20 minutes and wasting both your and the candidate's time.

A phone interview is an easy way to make sure that the candidate is truly interested and has the experience and qualifications you're looking for. **But there's a step you should take before you do a phone interview.**

I call this step, deal breakers.

Deal Breakers

Deal breakers are the reason you can't or won't extend a job offer to someone. It's also the reason people can't or won't accept your job offer. For every position you consider hiring, you likely have at least two to three deal breakers. Common deal breakers are:

For Employers

- ⚡ Compensation
- ⚡ Lack of required licensures
- ⚡ Inability to pass a pre-employment check like a background check, DMV screening, drug test, etc.
- ⚡ Lack of experience in a similar role
- ⚡ Lack of experience with software and tools used in the role.

For Candidates

- ⚡ Compensation or pay rate
- ⚡ Benefits (or lack thereof)
- ⚡ Commute or location of office
- ⚡ No upward career growth opportunities
- ⚡ Limited vacation or PTO.

These are just some of the most common deal breakers. I'm willing to bet you can think of a few reasons you've decided not to hire quickly and why people have declined your job offers in the past.

Address deal breakers *before* the phone interview OR at the very beginning of the phone interview.

I recommend reaching out over email to set up interviews. It is faster and easier than playing phone tag.

There are templates for setting up interviews in the Hiring Toolkit. Feel free to make them your own.

If you're waiting to go over the deal breakers on the phone interview, here is how I usually start the conversation:

"I just want to go over a couple of things to make sure I don't waste your time or mine, so we're just going to review some things right off the bat."

Deal Breaker #1 – Are you okay working Saturdays?

Deal Breaker #2 – How far are you from (the location they will be working at)?

Deal Breaker #3 – Compensation. Yes, I know you read somewhere that you shouldn't talk about compensation until everyone is sure everyone understands the job and the expectations. The simple reality is, if your compensation is $10,000 less than what they are making now, most people won't or simply can't take that big of a paycut. Some people can't even afford to take a $2,000 pay cut, which is about $1 an hour. Likewise, you can't afford to fall in love with the "champagne" candidate when you're on a "beer" budget. Did you follow that? Or was it just me whose mom always said, "Rikka, you have champagne taste on a beer budget" when I was growing up?

Almost everyone has gone through an interview process only to get an offer at the end that is much less than they expected or are willing to consider. When companies (and candidates) don't talk about money upfront, they often end up wasting each other's time. Frankly, you're too busy to waste time interviewing people you can't afford. There is nothing good that comes from being afraid to talk about money early.

HOW TO

TALK ABOUT MONEY

So, how much money do you make?

It's definitely not cocktail party conversation. But, it's a huge part of the hiring conversation. I am so comfortable talking to people about what they earn, I don't even get uncomfortable anymore. Here's a super-simple tip that will help you get more comfortable talking about money.

Start talking about money early, and talk about it often.

The more you do this, the better you will get at it, and the less time you will waste on people you can't afford. In the phone interview, start by simply asking:

"Just so I don't waste your time or mine, let's talk about compensation to make sure we aren't way off. What are you expecting in regards to a compensation to make a change? If that feels like a hard question to answer, simply think about what you're earning now and what you'd need to see to seriously consider an opportunity, and we can start with that to make sure we're not way off."

Yes, it's bold. Yes, some people will try to skirt the question and put it back on the opportunity. But, most people will be relieved to find out if they are in the right range or not. But, you must say it with conviction. If you squeak it out in a mousy voice, the more assertive candidates are going to walk all over you.

PRO TIP Many states and cities have made asking about salary history illegal, so be sure to focus on the future and their compensation expectations.

Sometimes people will "embellish" their compensation range. Sometimes it's because they are a lying jerk. Most of the time it's because they won't make a change unless it's an upward move. If you're expecting them to make about $50,000 and they say they are making $77,000, you have three options:

1. Let them know it's probably too far away to continue the conversation. Sometimes they will say, "Oh, how far off? I have some flexibility."

2. Trust your gut. If they feel like a lying jerk, just say, "Hey, thanks so much for your time, but we are probably too far off for this position to interest you." Hang up and move on.

Most of the time they're not going to lie; they're going to say, "Right now I am making $42,000 a year. I have a 15% bonus, and I've made it the last three years. It's not guaranteed, but that's what I usually get, so that probably is something that I would need to have in consideration to make a change."

I know, it's bold and probably a little scary for some of you. But it is a huge time saver, and it takes away the guessing and hoping they'll accept your offer out of the mix.

So, how do you talk money? Here's an example:

In the very first interview, once you've determined if they have the qualifications for the job, you simply ask:

"What are you looking for with regards to compensation in your next position?"
OR
"What would you be expecting to earn in a position like this?"

Then be quiet.

Chances are very good the candidate will give you a vague answer like:

"Well, it depends on the position."
OR
"I am sure you will put together a fair offer."

So, then you can ask:

"Okay, so what are you making now?"
OR
"Well, our range for this position is between $18-$21 an hour. Does that work for you?"

Then be quiet.

The key part of this process is the "be quiet" sections. You know the saying, "the first one to talk loses"? Same thing here. Trust me, they're as uncomfortable as you are. Just ride it out and reap the rewards.

Money isn't the entire decision for most people, but it's certainly a major consideration. Be alert to any changes in their situation. Counter offers from their current employer or another job opportunity can make a $40,000 person into a $45,000 person overnight. If you get a feeling that something has shifted, just ask them if they're still interested in the opportunity. You will be pleasantly surprised at how effective being direct can be.

Tip: *If you're prepared to pay between $16-$24 an hour, don't share the top end of your range. Once they hear it, they start thinking they deserve that amount. I try to leave myself a range of $2-$3 per hour. It is much better for them to have the impression your range is $16-$20 an hour and you went to $22/hour for them, rather than thinking they **only got** $22/ hour and they could have gotten $24/hour.*

Once you've gotten your deal breakers answered, it's always a good practice to see if they have anything that might be a deal killer on their end. This is done by simply saying:

"Okay, great, everything sounds good on my end. Is there anything you want to share or ask me right off the bat that may be a deal killer for you?"

WARNING: Some candidates take this as a time to ask you 112 questions about the job. If they do that, simply say we'll get more into the details in a bit, but right now I'm just wondering if you have any other job opportunities that are nearing an offer, or if you have some deal breaker items on your end you want to cover right away.

The reason you ask about opportunities that are nearing an offer is to find out if you have competition and to find out if they need to make a decision soon. It is always good to know if they have other opportunities in the pipeline so you don't miss out on the candidates you want because you moved too slow between interviews and lost them to a fast-moving competitor.

PRO TIP *Typically, I like to keep it to three deal breakers, because it gets a little awkward if you have seven deal breakers. "And another thing that sucks…" We don't want to do that. Think about the top three things you need, and the top three things they might say no to. With that, you will be talking to people who are more likely to say yes.*

How to Rock the Phone Interview

Phone interviews are awesome. They can also be awful if they're done poorly, so let's avoid doing it awkardly and set you up for success using this powerful interviewing tool.

Be Prepared

⚡ Print off their resume and review it.

⚡ Identify areas of interest you want to discuss in more detail.

⚡ Have your candidate ranking sheet printed off and ready to go. Just five minutes before the interview is enough time to settle yourself and organize your thoughts. Go to the bathroom, refill your coffee, do whatever you need to do to be centered and present in the moment.

Set the Stage

We all like a program when we go to an event. It helps us understand the flow and be prepared for each stage (and know where we are in the process).

Start the interview by simply letting them know you'll be going over some potential deal breakers in the interest of not wasting their time or yours. Then you will want to walk through their resume from the beginning of their career until now so you can understand their full career progression. As you go through their work history, you may ask some more detailed questions about experiences that tie closely to the role they are interviewing for. Once that's done, you'll answer any questions they have and let them know what the next steps will be.

The more clearly you set the stage for the interview flow, the more likely it is to be a successful and efficient interview. If you set the stage and the candidate doesn't respect it or is kind of a jerk about answering questions from their experience in the 90's, you're getting great insight into how they will handle any process that isn't done the way they want it done.

Establish Rapport and Create Connection

Everyone's a little nervous at the start of an interview. Call it nerves, excitement, whatever … everyone knows this could be the start of something big. Respect that and spend the first few minutes establishing rapport. Talk about the weather, the traffic, weekend plans. Better interviews happen when everyone is comfortable.

Everyone uses the "Tell Me About Yourself" interview question, but great interviewers use it to create a connection with the candidate.

For example:

I grew up in a tiny town in North Dakota, so if anyone has anything to do with North Dakota, (even if they've just watched the movie *Fargo*, which was set in Minnesota, by the way…) we have a connection. I've talked about the movie *Fargo* with about 5,000 people, and I doubt I've ever seen the whole thing, but it creates a connection with strangers.

Try to create that connection in the first few minutes of the interview. It will lead to a more natural and authentic conversation and a better understanding of the candidate.

Confirm Their Experience

The point of a phone interview is to clearly find out if they have the skills and experience to be successful in the role. It's not a good way to find out if they are a great cultural fit, but you will get many clues about that, too. Ask a series of functional questions regarding their experience as it relates to your business.

For instance, if you're looking for someone in sales and marketing, ask them specific questions about what they've sold in the past, whether they've ever developed a marketing strategy from scratch, if they've ever managed a sales team, etc.

For instance, if it is essential that they know how to use your ERP system, but it isn't listed on their resume, ask about it now. If they don't know it, and you won't have the time to train them, it's on to the next candidate.

I don't care how nice a person is if they can't do the job I need them to do. The last thing I want to do is put a nice person into a job they are going to fail at. Straight talk about the role and responsibilities is crucial to making the best hires.

Be sure to download your Candidate Ranking Sheet from the Hiring Toolkit and print off several copies to make comparing candidates easy.

HOW TO

CONDUCT A
PHONE INTERVIEW

Once I've confirmed I'm talking to the right person and it's still a good time for them to talk, I go right into "business" mode.

1. I cover any deal breakers that haven't been addressed.

2. I share the highlights about the company and the opportunity.

3. I ask them to "Tell Me About Yourself" (and I look for a connection).

4. Now the interview really starts. I ask the candidate to walk me through their work history.

I simply say:

"Okay, what I want to do is to get a better understanding of your work history and some of your career highlights. So, what we're going to do is start at the bottom of your resume and work our way up to current day. For each company I want you to tell me a bit about the company, what you did there, some of your successes, and ultimately why you moved on. I may jump in with specific questions from time to time, but for the most part I just want to get a thorough understanding of your career progression. So, let's start with (first job on resume — hopefully, the earliest in their career)…"

Then we do exactly that. The best candidates can pretty much walk you through their entire career without needing prompts or reminders to answer the four main things you want to know about.

1. The company – what kind of company was it (so you have the right context)?

2. Their role – what did they do at the company?

3. What were some of their successes?

4. Why did they ultimately leave?

You will need to remind or prompt most candidates a couple of times to get them in the flow of answering all four questions at once. But, most candidates get in the flow after the first company or two.

At any time you can interrupt their answer to ask specific questions.

"Sorry, I just want to dig in a bit deeper about this …"

"Sorry, I just want to make sure I understood that correctly, this is what I got from it (repeat what you understood). Is that correct or am I off?"

"Oh, that's interesting. Let's go into more detail about that …"

Once the candidate has walked you through their work history, you may have all the answers you need at this point. You may have already decided they weren't going to be a good fit, or they were amazing and you wanted to bring them in for a face-to-face. You can make a decision at this point and move to close the interview.

However, if you're still not sure if they're qualified or worth bringing in for a face-to-face interview, ask several functional questions to help you get clear on their ability to do the job. It's okay to keep asking questions until you're sure.

FUNCTIONAL
Interview Questions

These questions are focused on what the individual has done in the past and usually only require a "yes" or "no" answer. However, savvy interviewers know that valuable information can be gained by asking a functional interview question and then asking follow-up questions to get a clear understanding of the candidate's level of knowledge and experience.

Don't forget to ask the follow-up questions to each.

General Examples

⚡ Have you ever had profit and loss responsibility for a $3 million budget?

⚡ Have you ever done retail or inside sales?

⚡ Have you used QuickBooks?

Management

⚡ Have you ever managed a team of people?

⚡ Have you ever had to provide corrective action or disciplinary action to an employee?

⚡ Have you ever had to fire someone?

Sales and Marketing Questions

⚡ Have you ever developed a marketing plan?

⚡ Have you ever sold "this"?

⚡ Have you ever sold to "this type of customer"?

⚡ Have you ever sold through "this channel"?

Get a download of these functional interview questions in the Hiring Toolkit.

Be Curious and Ask Follow-up Questions

The No. 1 way to improve your interviewing results is to be curious and ask follow-up questions to get the information you need.

The 10 questions you planned to ask are NOT your entire interview. They are jumping off points for conversation and dialogue so you truly understand what the candidate is bringing to the table.

Actually listen to their answers.

Duh, right? But, in this case, I want you to be listening like a recruiter. You're listening for potential objections, concerns, or other things that may make the deal fall apart. You want to address those concerns if you can. For example, if they have left their last four jobs because they had to work Saturday mornings, your job that requires working Saturdays is most likely going to end the same way.

Likewise, be listening for "selling points." If your opening doesn't require weekends, that is a bonus in your favor. If their current boss is a micro-manager and stifling them, the fact that you are a hands-off manager who expects results but doesn't hover is going to be a major selling point.

Above all ...
TRUST YOUR GUT.

What?! We've all heard "hire with your head" and that "gut instinct" is a path to disaster. Well, I say bullshit. I believe deeply in the power of intuition and "gut instinct" when hiring. If everything looks good on paper, but something feels wrong in the interview — trust that. Don't talk yourself into hiring someone if it doesn't feel right.

Now, there is a caveat. If you've previously had problems hiring, you will want to make sure your "gut instinct" isn't just fear of being wrong again.

Close the Interview

After you've gotten the information, you need to determine if the person is worth bringing to the next level. You have a couple of choices. If you aren't sure if they should go to the next level, ask any follow-up questions to get the information you need. But, if you are just on the fence, say something like:

"I have several more interviews this week, so I will be in touch when I decide who is moving on to the next step."

If you are sure they aren't going forward, you can verbally reject them (this is for when you are very comfortable interviewing):

"Thanks so much for your time today. We've been fortunate to have several qualified applicants for this position and, unfortunately, I don't think your experience will put you in the top three that will move on to the next step. I will keep you in mind should anything change or a position that's a better fit opens up."

If you are interested in them, let them know when you would like to do the next interview and, ideally, get it scheduled when you are on the phone with them.

chapter thirteen

Face-*to*-Face
Interview

Now, it's getting serious. We like the candidate enough to invite them back for a more detailed conversation in person. This is often the first time they will see your office, so make sure you're prepared.

Face-to-face interviews are where we start to dig in to see if they are going to be able to do the job and fit in. This is where behavioral and situational interviews come into play. I'm going to include several ways for you to take your interviewing up a notch.

· ·

PRO TIP *If possible, schedule your face-to-face interviews on or close to the same day. This will make your comparison of candidates more effective. It is important to take notes during the interview and then use your candidate ranking sheet to note highlights or concerns about the candidate. Once you have completed all your interviews, you will have accurate information on each candidate to review as you decide who will advance to the next step or who will receive an offer.*

· ·

HOW TO

USE VIDEO INTERVIEWS

One of the bright sides of COVID-19 has been the huge surge in the use of video interviews in the LBM Industry. I've been advocating for them for years, but chances are your organization just discovered how powerful they can be during the global pandemic.

There are many options you can use to conduct video interviews. It largely depends on the communication platforms your business has chosen to use.

Here is a list of some of the most popular and easy to use video interview platforms:

- ⚡ Zoom.us
- ⚡ Microsoft Teams
- ⚡ Google Meet
- ⚡ Skype
- ⚡ FaceTime

BEHAVIORAL
Interview Questions

Behavioral interview questions have long been a favorite of HR managers and hiring managers. The idea behind them is that they give you a glimpse into the job applicant's work ethic, their approach to challenges, and their ability to work as a team.

These are great questions to ask during a face-to-face interview.

Behavioral interview questions can't stand alone though.

They need you to be an active listener who asks for clarification or qualification until you understand. Often, the greatest value comes from outside the scope of their actual answer.

The key to behavioral interview questions is that they ask about a SPECIFIC example or situation. Here are some examples:

- Tell me about a time that you went above and beyond for a customer.
- Give me an example of a time that a co-worker frustrated you and how you handled it.
- Describe a situation when you had to resolve conflict in the workplace.
- Tell me about a time you had to convince someone to complete a task your way or to do something they didn't want to do.
- Tell me about a time you set a goal and achieved it.
- Tell me about a time you set a goal and DIDN'T achieve it.
- Tell me about the best boss you've ever had. (Then as a follow-up question: Tell me about a specific thing you remember that had a positive impact on you.)
- Tell me about a time you had to make a difficult decision.

As you can see, behavioral interview questions set the stage for job applicants to tell you about their skills, their experience, and their approach. All of these can be very helpful in determining their fit for the job.

However, I think the greatest value of a behavioral interview question is that many people don't actually answer the question you asked. For example:

Question: *Tell me about a time that you went above and beyond for a customer.*

Response: *Well, at ABC Company we prided ourselves on the customer always being right. It allowed me to really go above and beyond in many ways.*

Do you see the problem?

The response doesn't actually answer the question. It was a nice, articulate response — but skirted the actual question being asked.

The true value of behavioral questions is that you get an insider view of whether they will actively listen and follow instructions. Most people — around 70% to 80% — will give a specific answer once you ask the question a second time. However, there is a section of the population that truly believes they are answering the question, and they will begin to get annoyed with you because you are asking them the same thing repeatedly. That, my friend, is a pretty clear sign that they are often going to have trouble following your instructions and probably not someone you want to hire.

SITUATIONAL
Interview Questions

Though not as well-known as functional and behavioral interview questions, situational interview questions are my favorite tool for predicting future behavior.

They require job-seekers to respond to a specific hypothetical situation they may face on the job. Like behavioral-based interview questions, situational interview questions are designed to "short-circuit" memorized answers and force the applicant to think on their feet.

The main difference between behavioral and situational interview questions is that behavioral questions are focused on the past and situational questions are focused on the future.

When done correctly, both behavioral and situational interview questions can give you a sense of a potential hire's personality, work experience, thought process, and communication skills, which is about as good as it gets in interviewing.

For you to get the most value from your situational interview questions, you must break away from canned interview questions and really think about the position you are trying to fill and develop specific questions. I know that can feel a bit daunting, so I've included a few examples to get you started.

Examples of Situational Interview Questions

⚡ **Multi-tasking**
"A customer is walking in, the phone is ringing, and a co-worker needs help making a copy. Walk me through how you'd handle these competing needs for your attention."

⚡ Sales client relationships

"Walk me through how you would build a relationship with a prospect. How would you take them from not knowing who we are and move them to being interested in our product?"

⚡ Customer relationships and retention

"How would you handle a client who was angry with you over something that wasn't your fault?"

⚡ Employee management

"Let's pretend you have an employee whom everyone loves on the team. She's has great energy and is a ton of laughs. Unfortunately, she is also missing her activity goals weekly. She always has a good reason for it, and after you meet with her, it seems like she is going to really focus next week and hit them, but she always falls short. How would you handle this 'great' employee's poor performance?"

⚡ Supervising

"If you were hiring a new employee for (fill in a role they'd be supervising), walk me through how you'd go about setting and communicating activity and performance expectations."

The power of situational interviewing is that it impedes the candidate's ability to respond with cookie-cutter answers. The more creative and specific you are with your hypothetical situations, the more you'll get to see your potential employee's thought process in action. If you take some time to think about situations that come up in the role and tailor your questions around those, you'll end up with a far stronger understanding of the candidates for the role.

PRO TIP *Here is a key question: "Tell me a little bit about what you did (at ABC Company) and ultimately why you decided to move on." This is a subtle way to find out if they can follow instructions and provide the "right" amount of information and the "right" information in a professional setting.*

It's crucial that you don't get stuck in sales mode and forget to screen for fit and ability. **One of the largest challenges when you're hiring for your company is to stop selling.**

STOP **SELLING**

It can feel intensely personal when interviewing for your team or company. Let's not kid ourselves — interviewing is a bit like dating. We want to be the ones who are in the position to "reject" someone. This desire can subconsciously lead us to focus on selling vs. qualifying.

It may feel uncomfortable for you to drill down and ask probing questions during the interview. Don't worry. If your tone and demeanor are friendly and engaging, most people won't even realize you're probing into their answers. Unless, of course, they are lying. The liars are going to get uncomfortable when you begin to poke holes in their story.

Always keep in mind, hiring is a business decision, and it's a big one. You need to have confidence in your decision, and confidence comes from having solid information. Should you choose to be timid and accept everything at face value, it may work out. But chances are it will result in an underperforming or pain-in-the-neck employee you'll have to terminate.

INTERVIEW QUESTIONS
TO GET YOU STARTED

⚡ Who was your favorite manager and why?

⚡ What kind of personality do you work best with and why?

⚡ Why do you want this job?

⚡ Tell me about your proudest achievement.

⚡ If you were at a business lunch and you ordered a rare steak and they brought it to you well done, what would you do?

⚡ How would you go about establishing your credibility quickly with the team?

⚡ There's no right or wrong answer, but if you could be anywhere in the world right now, where would you be?

⚡ How would you feel about working for someone who knows less than you?

⚡ Was there a person in your career who really made a difference?

⚡ What's your ideal company?

⚡ What attracted you to this company?

⚡ What are you most proud of?

⚡ What are you looking for in terms of career development?

⚡ What do you look for in terms of culture — structured or entrepreneurial?

⚡ What do you like to do?

⚡ Give examples of ideas you've had or implemented.

⚡ What do you ultimately want to become?

⚡ How would you describe your work style?

- Tell me about a time where you had to deal with conflict on the job.

- What's the last book you read?

- What would be your ideal working situation?

- Why should we hire you?

- What did you like least about your last job?

- What do you think of your previous/current boss?

- What can you do for us that other candidates can't?

- What are three positive things your last boss would say about you?

- What's one negative thing would your last boss say about you?

- How do you want to improve yourself in the next year?

- What were the responsibilities of your last position?

- What do you know about this industry?

- What do you know about our company?

- How long will it take for you to make a significant contribution?

- What was the last project you headed up, and what was its outcome?

- What kind of goals would you have in mind if you got this job?

- Give me an example of a time that you felt you went above and beyond the call of duty at work.

- Can you describe a time when your work was criticized?

- Have you ever been on a team where someone was not pulling their own weight? How did you handle it?

- Tell me about a time when you had to give someone difficult feedback. How did you handle it?

⚡ What is your greatest failure, and what did you learn from it?

⚡ What irritates you about other people, and how do you deal with it?

⚡ What is your greatest fear?

⚡ Who has impacted you most in your career, and how?

⚡ What do you see yourself doing within the first 30 days of this job?

⚡ What's the most important thing you've learned in school?

⚡ What three character traits would your friends use to describe you?

⚡ What will you miss about your present/last job?

⚡ If you were interviewing someone for this position, what traits would you look for?

⚡ List five words that describe your character.

⚡ What is your greatest achievement outside of work?

⚡ Sell me this pencil.

⚡ If I were your supervisor and asked you to do something that you disagreed with, what would you do?

⚡ Do you think a leader should be feared or liked?

⚡ What's the most difficult decision you've made in the last two years?

⚡ What do you like to do for fun?

⚡ Why are you leaving your present job?

⚡ What do you do in your spare time?

⚡ How do you feel about taking no for an answer?

⚡ What was the most difficult period in your life, and how did you deal with it?

- ⚡ What is your favorite memory from childhood?

- ⚡ Give me an example of a time you did something wrong. How did you handle it?

- ⚡ Tell me one thing about yourself you wouldn't want me to know.

- ⚡ Tell me the difference between good and exceptional.

- ⚡ Why did your choose your major?

- ⚡ What are the qualities of a good leader? A bad leader?

- ⚡ What is your biggest regret, and why?

- ⚡ What assignment was too difficult for you, and how did you resolve the issue?

- ⚡ If I were to ask your last supervisor to provide you additional training or exposure, what would she suggest?

- ⚡ If you could choose one superhero power, what would it be and why?

- ⚡ What's the best movie you've seen in the last year?

- ⚡ Describe how you would handle a situation if you were required to finish multiple tasks by the end of the day, and there was no conceivable way that you could finish them.

- ⚡ What techniques and tools do you use to keep yourself organized?

- ⚡ If you had to choose one, would you consider yourself a big-picture person or a detail-oriented person?

- ⚡ If selected for this position, can you describe your strategy for the first 90 days?

- ⚡ Who are your heroes?

 There is a PDF download of 100 interview questions in the Hiring Toolkit.

chapter fourteen

Choosing
with
CONFIDENCE

Interviews are great tools, but sometimes you still want more information before you make your decision. Using pre-employment assessments and tests can help you to make sure your No. 1 candidate is "the one."

(Note: although this is still part of the selection process, these steps are usually reserved for candidates in the final stages.)

Almost all large businesses use some level of pre-employment assessment or test before hiring employees, but very few small businesses know how to effectively use these tools to help them hire better.

Pre-employment assessments or self-assessments can be powerful selection tools, but they can also easily be misused.

Assessments should never be used **exclusively** to rule people out.

They are a tool, not something that should be used to decide someone's fate.

I also believe the greatest power in assessments may come by helping the hiring manager learn more about themselves and how they are showing up to their employees (and probably the world in general).

Here are a few things I know about myself:

I'm high-energy. I thrive on change. I can be (very) direct. Sometimes I talk over people.

I didn't learn these things from the comment section of my grade-school report card or because a friend diplomatically pointed them out. I learned them by clicking boxes in a variety of assessments.

While some view interview personality tests as a waste of time, the truth is that the right personality assessment can give you in-depth knowledge about a potential employee. A good assessment will also tell you where your potential hire's strengths and interests lie, which helps you identify tasks that truly excite and interest them.

Still, we're all a little fascinated with the inner workings of our own brains, right? I mean, there's a reason those "Which Game of Thrones Character Are You?" online self-assessments are so popular! Luckily for us, those personality quizzes, intelligence assessments, and employment tests can make us better business owners and managers.

Why You Should Use Assessments

1. They make us aware of our own habits.

Now that I know my high energy and love of change can tire my team out, I can share that information with potential hires. I can "prepare" them and let them know that it's totally okay to ask me to slow down or tell me that they need a break or more turnaround time. When we spend all this time hiring someone, we want to make sure they're totally prepared for what they're getting into and the quirks of everyone they're working with — including us!

2. They tell us more about our hires.

Some tests include a manager's report. This version of the test results is written for a manager who is considering hiring someone. It gives insight into their issues, struggles, and personality so you can see how you match up. Even better, with this information you can create behavioral interview questions based on their assessment results:

It sounds like you like being the leader. Tell me about a time when you weren't the leader and how that went.

It looks like you're very meticulous and detail-oriented. Tell me about a time you had a very tight deadline and how you dealt with that.

3. They help us turn high potential into high performing.

A good assessment will also tell you where your potential hire's strengths and interests lie, which helps you identify tasks that truly excite and interest them. If they're super social, give them more public-facing duties. If they'd like to do more creative work, put them in charge of designing images for social media. When you give employees tasks related to their interests, they're so much more likely to stay engaged and give you more value for your payroll dollar.

4. They help us hire better.

Most tools have a "success profile" built in for a wide variety of roles, but, TTI Success Insights, the assessment provider we use actually has a patented job benchmarking process that let's the job talk. Of course you can also use your top performers, if you prefer.

Choosing the Right Assessment

As a headhunter, I've worked with dozens of different pre-hire employment assessments. I'm now a proud partner of TTI Success Insights® (TTI SI), the world's leading developer of research-based, validated behavioral assessments that enable organizations to use the **Science of Self™** to reveal and harness the talent and skills of their greatest asset — their people. You can learn more about your assessment options at BuildingGurus.com/assessments. Depending on how deep you want to dive in, the cost per assessment can vary from $50 to several hundred dollars.

I love that TTI SI combines the best of many assessment tools into one. I'm going to briefly go over the five dimensions of a superior performer that can be measured by TTI SI's research-based assessments: Behaviors, 12 Driving Forces, Acumen, Competencies, and Emotional Intelligence (EQ).

Behaviors

Success in life, work, and relationships stems from understanding and having a sense of self — of deeply comprehending who you are, what you do, and how you do it.

The research-based, validated TTI SI measures behaviors in five behavioral dimensions using the DISC theory. DISC measures Dominance, Influence, Steadiness, and Compliance and was first developed by William Moulton Marston.

The Behaviors/DISC assessment is key to helping people understand HOW they behave and their ability to interact effectively with others in work and life.

12 Driving Forces

Whereas behaviors illustrate the HOW of our actions and decision-making, motivators explain the WHY behind your actions and passions.

12 Driving Forces, based on Eduard Spranger's theory of human motivation, are the windows through which an individual views the world. These intrinsic motivations explain the key driving forces about someone's on-the-job performance and why they act a certain way.

Acumen

Possessing a high level of acumen means someone has the ability to make good judgments and quick decisions due to their natural abilities and/or capacities.

A person's acumen — or keenness and depth of perception or discernment — is directly related to his or her level of performance. The stronger a person's acumen, the more aware that person is of their reality.

Competencies

While not every job requires the development of all 25 competencies, TTI SI examines 25 different personal skills. For many jobs, it's not always the technical skills that will catapult employees to success, but rather the personal skills, or "soft skills," that are often transferable to different jobs.

In the workplace, it's these intangible, indefinable soft skills, such as leadership, persuasion, and playing well with others, that complement one's technical knowledge. These are the qualities that define us as people and are typically bottom line indicators of employee job performance.

Emotional Intelligence (EQ)

The ability to understand one's own and other people's emotions in the decision-making process is critical in facilitating high levels of collaboration and productivity and achieving superior performance in the workplace.

With rapidly changing conditions in the business world, individuals with high emotional intelligence (EQ) have greater mental health, exemplary job performance and strong leadership skill.

Choosing with Confidence

Sometimes you still want more information before you make your decision. Here are some additional tools you can use:

Skill Testing

Skill testing is the modern version of a typing test. The applicant uses the software they are being evaluated on in a test environment. Their score is tabulated and shared with potential employers. Skill testing is commonly used by temporary staffing firms to verify the skill level an applicant has before sending them to the client site. Independent contractor sites like Upwork may also offer contractors a way to test their skills and showcase their results on their profile. If you're planning on hiring directly and your position requires an advanced level understanding of office software like Word, Excel, or Outlook, your local job service may administer the tests for you or you can find providers online by Googling what you need. This is a great step to use if you've been misled in the past about how strong someone's skills are.

Pre-Hire Projects

Use pre-hire projects to assess someone's skill and experience level. You simply create a hypothetical project for the candidate to work on. You provide all the details they will need, clear expectations, and a timeline. The candidate then turns the completed project in to you and you're able to review their work. These trial runs work wonderfully when you need to be sure the candidate can do the job to the level you expect. This works well with marketing positions, administrative positions, and anything that can be bundled into a small project.

❗ WARNING: Don't make the project overly time-consuming. The project should take less than an hour or two to complete. If you give them a project that will take too long, you're likely to lose their interest. You also need to be mindful that it isn't perceived as trying to get work done for free. If most of your projects take hours to complete, just use a small part of the project to assess their abilities.

PRO TIP *If you take the time to set up a pre-hire project for a role with your company, be sure to save it so you can use it again in the future. You may just want to create a Pre-Hire Project folder and save them all in the same location.*

Ride Along / A Day in the Life

A "ride along" is a chance for you or a member of your current team to spend an extended amount of time with the candidate outside of the typical interview setting. The typical use of a ride along is for outside sales roles. The candidate spends the day going with you or an existing rep on cold calls, sales calls, etc. The more casual setting and the length of time you spend together helps you to get a better feel for how they will perform on calls, and helps the candidate get a better feel for the job.

Use this for positions where you want the candidate to know what they're signing up for. Call centers and other businesses with high turnover will benefit from giving someone a taste of the job before they hire and train them.

chapter fifteen

Before Extending *the* OFFER

Getting ready to make your big move and hire someone is an exciting time. But, this is a big decision, and there are additional steps you may want to take to ensure that you're making the best possible choice, as well as protecting yourself and your business.

Reference Checks

I believe in the power of the interview. I think there's more value in interviewing, doing assessments, testing skills, and developing pre-hire projects than in calling a reference. I think an interview, when done well, tells you pretty much everything you need to know about your candidate.

At a bare minimum, your interview should tell you if they are smart enough to give you a reference from someone who's going to say something positive about them. If you interview somebody and like them enough to get their references, and then they give you somebody who bashes them, you have failed at the interview process.

Pretty much everyone in the world knows that you should choose references who are going to say positive things about you. If you were wow'd enough to check references and they stink, you need to take a serious look at your interview process because it needs some significant improvement.

Assume most references are going to be positive. Be sure to weigh that positive review with the fact that the candidate hand-picked this person to say nice things about them. Chances are they evolved from co-workers to friends over the years, which means they are easy to work with. However, you can't be sure they weren't the two talking at the water cooler for an hour each day.

Some references are from jobs or positions they held years ago. Before you waste your time checking these references, make sure the experience is relevant to what you are currently hiring them for. If they were a vet tech before they went back to school for accounting, does their bedside manner with animals matter to you?

Some might argue that reference checks are important in finding out if a candidate is lying about credentials. I absolutely agree that verification is important. But these days, there are online programs that verify employment and education credentials. They are inexpensive and much more accurate than calling a number the candidate gives you for a company that may or may not exist anymore.

Frankly, reference checks lost their value eons ago. They lost their value because there's so much litigation and liability that nobody's going tell you anything anyway. In my opinion, the half hour to an hour you might spend doing reference checks is essentially a waste of time. You would be much better off spending time doing something else. Like having a cup of coffee with a key employee.

The Backdoor Reference

There is a temptation to check "back door references" and contact your own sources within the scope of the candidate's resume. On the surface, that sounds like a smart call — searching for outside references could allow you to find out what you need to know. Look deeper and the real value-versus-risk comes to light. Unless you're in a very rare situation, the risk you take when you violate confidentiality during the interview process is a risk to your goodwill and legal liability. It isn't worth the potential headaches. Once you're ready to extend an offer, you can get the candidate's permission to check with your contacts. Just don't do it behind their back.

Why not do guerilla reference checks?

You won't know the difference between truth and gossip. You don't know the relationship dynamics. The backdoor source may not have worked closely with your candidate or may have had a personal dislike or issue with them. The source may not understand the role or the experience to judge the candidate properly. Some "backdoor" reference sources are quick to tell you they don't know enough about the person to give solid feedback, but some people are excited to pass on anything they've heard — true or not.

Also, if you are talking about a connection from more than a few years ago, keep in mind: would you like someone to judge your 24-year-old self for a job you're going to have at the age of 32?

Candidates (especially passive seekers) don't appreciate the breach of confidentiality during the hiring process nor are they comfortable with the ethics you show by digging for sources behind their back. Deals and contract negotiations have been ended over less.

In short, checking backdoor references sounds good but skilled interviewers can get far more information and a much better picture of a candidate's skills, strengths, and weaknesses, without any risks.

Background Checks

Are you running background checks on new hires? If you aren't, **you should be.**

According to the Society of Human Resource Management, 37% of all applicants put some false information on their applications and 65% of resumes are enhanced or exaggerated.

I get it. It might seem too complicated or pricey to run these kinds of tests on every fresh face joining your team. You want to believe you're a good judge of character, and that you wouldn't make the mistake of hiring a person with a tendency to stick their hand in the petty cash.

However, this is one of those instances where what you don't know can cost you — and hurt your business in a *major way.*

Don't think you need to run a background check because your prospective employee won't be dealing with cash? Think again. Your liability as an owner goes much further than petty cash. Lawsuits for "negligent hiring" have been on the rise.

To give you an idea of how far your liability can go:

A pizza company hired a delivery driver without considering his criminal past, which included a sexual assault conviction and arrest for stalking a woman he met while delivering pizza for another company. After he raped a customer, the pizza franchise was liable to the victim for negligent hiring.

It has been proven time and time again that companies with background check policies have fewer employee thefts and violence issues than companies without them.

HOW TO

RUN A BACKGROUND CHECK

I've worked with a lot of different background check providers, most of them require huge volume purchases to get any level of customer service. I like GoodHire. They are actively trying to help the small employer. Some of the larger background check providers just don't seem interested in businesses with less than 50 employees.

For around $55 you can get: A social security number trace and address history (this verifies their SSN, names, aliases, and addresses for verification process) plus a National Criminal Databases search (used to find felony or serious misdemeanor convictions), a County Criminal Court check (used to obtain court records that haven't been digitized yet), a Sex Offender List check, and a Domestic Terrorist Watch List check.

For $79 you can get a report that includes education and employment verification. You can also add on items like a Motor Vehicle Records check ($15) or a Professional License check ($15).

You can check out your options by going to www.BuildingGurus. com/goodhire (if you go this way, I'll get a little commission for introducing you to the brand, but you won't pay anymore), otherwise you can just go to www.Goodhire.com directly.

You can complete a very robust check on a potential hire for less than $100. Consider it money well-spent, because that would buy you about 30 minutes of your attorney's time if something bad did happen.

Types of Screening

Drug screening

The idea of incorporating pre-employment drug testing into your selection process is to lessen the impact of drug abuse on your business.

A few examples of how drug use can impact businesses: tardiness, absenteeism, turnover, attitude problems, decreased productivity, theft, crime, and violence.

While there are many reasons to incorporate drug screening, it's largely a simple way to improve your bottom line and lower your liability.

According to the U.S. Department of Labor, 65% of all on the job accidents are related to drug or alcohol use. Substance abusers are six times more likely to file workers comp claims than non-abusers.

. . . .

PRO TIP *It's a big red flag when you come upon a prospective hire who hesitates to continue when they learn a drug screening is part of your process. Now, on the other hand, if getting applicants past the drug screen is an issue for your organization (yes, this really is a problem in some industries!), try "fishing" in a different pond. Change up your recruiting sources to see if that helps. Also, be sure to include in bold in your job ad that a pre-employment drug test will be done and random drug testing will occur throughout employment. Make it easy for drug users to see this isn't a job they are going to have success with.*

. . . .

HOW TO

RUN A DRUG SCREENING

Courts have consistently upheld the liability of using drug screens in your selection process. Many employers see a huge benefit in conducting random drug tests.

Basic drug screens cost between $50 to $100 for most small employers. There are numerous companies with testing sites around the U.S. that you can contact to start the process. You can go to **www.BuildingGurus.com/goodhire** for additional information on drug screenings as well as background checks.

Protecting Yourself and Your Business

CYA
BEFORE YOU HIRE

Making the leap to employer is a pretty big deal. You have to think about how to protect your sanity, your reputation, and your assets. This may feel a bit overwhelming at first.

Employee Manual or Handbook

An employee manual is simply a document that spells out all your company's policies and procedures regarding employees. It's a fluid document and will change as your business grows and evolves. It's extremely important to have an employee manual that addresses any issues that may arise when you have employees.

PRO TIP *Many websites will offer to make an employee handbook for you for free, but you will need to buy it in order to download, save, or print it. This is super frustrating if you think you're building it for free and spend hours getting it ready only to be hit with the reality it is essentially worthless in its "free" form.*

Probationary Period

Typically, the new hire probationary period is 90 days. This means that for the first 90 days, you can terminate the employee for any reason. The probation period gives you an extended window of time to determine if the person will be able to succeed in the position. Generally, the terms of the probation period are spelled out in the employee handbook. Use this time to make sure the individual is a good fit in the role.

PRO TIP *Be sure to set realistic and achievable goals. First, this will set your candidate up for success. Everyone likes to be successful at their new job, so this is a great way for them to start off with a couple of wins. More importantly, this simple step will make it very clear to you if they aren't performing at the level you desire. Many entrepreneurs, myself included, have a high level of optimism. That optimism serves you well in most areas of your business. However, when assessing an employee's fit, tempered optimism is a better approach.*

Non-Competes / Confidentiality / Non-Solicitation Agreements

You want to protect your business's intellectual property and trade secrets. Depending on your state laws and business needs, you will choose a Non-Compete Agreement or a Confidentiality and Non-Solicitation Agreement.

A Non-Compete Agreement essentially states that the employee can't leave for a position that would put them in competition with their past employer. A Confidentiality and Non-Solicitation Agreement does more to protect your important business information, such as customer lists, pricing, and other trade secrets. It also states that the employee can't leave and then solicit your customers, prospects, or employees for a certain period of time.

How enforceable these agreements are varies widely from state to state, and from agreement to agreement, depending on the agreement language. Having your attorney draft an agreement that is specific to your state and industry will put you in the best possible position to defend it.

Here's an example of how non-competes can play out; Paul started working at ABC Company right after college in 1995. He'd been promoted a few times and was a top producing inside sales person. His compensation was a base of $35,000 with commission and bonus bringing him up to about $65,000 in total compensation. ABC's number one competitor was XYZ Corporation. They often competed for customers and projects. XYZ had been heavily recruiting Paul for years, but he'd never left ABC. Finally, in 2010 XYZ offered Paul a $30,000 increase in base salary, nearly doubling his base compensation. Paul accepted the offer from XYZ Corporation and gave notice at ABC Company. During the two weeks between when Paul gave his notice to ABC and when he was due to start at XYZ, ABC's legal team sent a letter to XYZ informing them that Paul had signed a non-compete in 1995 when he started. If Paul worked for XYZ, ABC intended to enforce the non-compete agreement. XYZ then chose to rescind their offer of employment to Paul instead of defending against the non-compete. By simply sending a letter to the new employer, ABC was able to stop one of their top sales people going to work for their competitor. This non-compete was 15 years old and still had the power to stop the candidate cold.

Generally, you would include your agreement in your employee handbook, but have it specifically signed by the employee. **Without this signed agreement, you can't enforce the terms. So, get it signed and keep it on file.**

Computer and Email Usage Agreement

This agreement spells out appropriate use of their work computer, Internet, and email. The basics such as: don't send dirty jokes from you work email address, don't visit porn sites, and don't use your work computer for nefarious activities.

At my first company, I had an employee who was a general pain in the ass, but I didn't have a clear reason to terminate him. Then he decided to send dirty jokes to his co-workers from his work email. Most of his co-workers also thought he sucked, so they told me about the dirty email. Because I had this agreement in place, I finally had cause to terminate him: He had been inappropriately using his work email. I simply pulled out the agreement, showed him where he had signed, and explained what he violated.

Again, this is typically included in the employee handbook, but is specifically signed by the employee.

WARNING: You may have heard the saying, "You can fire them if you don't like the color of their tie." Well, in right-to-work states that is true to some extent, but it is always a better practice to have a clear, defensible reason to terminate someone.

chapter sixteen

Extending *the* **OFFER**

Finally, you've done your interviews, crossed your t's and dotted your i's, and you're ready to extend an offer. Now all that is left is getting to "Yes!"

One of the advantages small businesses have in hiring is their flexibility. Keep this in mind and be creative to get the person you want.

> YOUR ABILITY TO CREATE A
> # WIN/WIN
> IS YOUR GREATEST STRENGTH.

Talking Money

Because you've been talking money since the beginning of the process, you know what the candidate is expecting. You also know that you can afford it.

Uh-oh. Were you too chicken to talk money before? In that case, you'd better put on your big kid pants now and pick up the phone. It should be a simple conversation:

Hey, Bob, it's Rikka from Building Gurus. I was just reviewing my notes on our conversation yesterday. It was so much fun talking to you that I forgot to find out about your salary requirements. So, what are you looking for in your next position?

If they give you an answer that's in your range, you can close the call warmly and get back to putting together the offer. If the amount is way off, you can simply say:

Okay, we were thinking around $40,000 for this position, so we're pretty far off. (Then be quiet.)

Depending on their level of interest in the role, they will either agree with you and the conversation will end, or they might say something like, "Well, I could probably make $40,000 work if I could work four 10-hour days or if I could telecommute two days a week."

Don't agree to or promise anything on this call. Simply take notes and let them know that you will be back in touch. Then consider the options and their ramifications before you put together an offer. **I would strongly encourage you to take a quick walk or a few deep breaths before you start crafting an offer that goes way outside of what you were expecting to present.**

This process can trigger your competitive nature, and you will want to "win" by getting up to their requirements. But you'd better make sure you're making a level-headed, business decision if you decide to go outside your parameters.

Talk It Over: Verbally Extend the Offer

Always verbally extend the offer first. Although doing this face to face gives you the best chance to read their reactions and non-verbal cues, realistically speaking, most verbal offers are made over the phone.

By verbally extending the offer, you give them a chance to ask questions and clarify things. You will also find out if there are any major issues. That way, you can address the problems before you send the formal written offer letter.

Be sure to keep the lines of communication open. It's better for your candidate to ask questions than for them to assume the issue is insurmountable and decline the offer.

The Offer Letter

A well-thought-out offer includes the following items:

- A warm and engaging opener
- The title of the position
- The address of where they will be working
- Compensation details
- Expected schedule or work hours
- An overview of the benefits package
- If possible, include what their out-of-pocket costs for the benefits will be
- A close with a deadline for an answer.

Be Prepared

You may have to compete against multiple offers or against a counter offer from their current employer. Even after they accept your offer, remember that the deal isn't done until they show up for work that first day.

Negotiating an offer is fairly common, so don't be offended if the candidate tries to negotiate with you. Obviously, money is the most commonly negotiated item, but other elements you can use to sweeten the pot are vacation days, flexible scheduling, telecommuting, etc. Be open-minded, but make sure you don't negotiate away everything.

Now, if they are kind of a dink during the negotiations and your interest in hiring them has pretty much disappeared, you can always rescind your offer. Basically, rescinding your offer is pulling it off the table. Even though you extended an employment offer, you don't have to hire them.

Let me tell you about one of the challenging searches I worked on. There weren't a lot of qualified candidates, but I did find one and my client liked him. I knew they were nearing an offer, but I was headed to Mexico for a vacation. I didn't expect the Internet to be an issue (after all, I had lived there). But, the first couple days we were there our Internet was sketchy at best. During this time, my client extended him an offer, which was an excellent offer. It was a 20% to 30% bump in total compensation. However, my candidate — likely with some cold feet about making a change and, I believe, largely because I wasn't available to walk him through the offer — got his feelings hurt because he wanted a substantial jump in base. The hiring manager decided that if the candidate didn't see the potential and the fact that we had already far exceeded what he was making, we were done with him. By the time my Internet situation was sorted out, they'd rescinded the offer. I joked to my husband that our vacation ended up costing about $20,000 more than we'd budgeted thanks to a lost deal.

My client was right to rescind it. If you are extending an offer to a sales person and they can't do the math on the numbers to recognize a huge bump in salary and the potential, you should rescind it. The candidate may still think that you'll get "desperate" enough to come back and give him a $15,000 bump in base, but you won't. By the time you rescind a search, it's over. The candidate has burned the bridge forever, in most cases.

I share this story, because sometimes negotiations are awkward. As a third-party recruiter, I believe this part of the process is where I usually earn my fee. I have the difficult and "get real" conversations with applicants and hiring managers and help everyone get to "yes." But, chances are you aren't paying a headhunter, so you will need to learn how to negotiate and figure out the real issues on your own.

My best advice to you is to be **straight forward**.

Don't bend and bend to meet candidate's requirements. You'll resent them before they even start. It never ends well.

WARNING: If you find yourself working really hard to "sell" a prospective employee, bending over backwards and promising them the moon — STOP. Take a deep breath and regroup. In my experience, the candidates that are the most demanding in the selection process or negotiations aren't likely to change. They will continue to expect you to make exceptions for them. If you've got your heart set on someone, be very, very sure they're worth the headaches they may cause.

PRO TIP *If they ask for longer than three days to make a decision on your offer, ask why. Typically, a delay of this length means they're waiting on another offer.*

IF THEY DECLINE YOUR OFFER

Sometimes, you just can't get to "yes." The important thing is to learn from the experience. Why didn't they accept the offer? How can you improve so that next time you don't have the same thing happen again?

Yes, it sucks when someone declines your offer. But, this is one of the best learning experiences in the hiring process.

I would encourage you to try to get past the ego part of having an offer declined and move into the learning part. What was going through the candidate's mind that made them say "no"? Ideally, you knew this might happen and you weren't completely blind-sided.

As a professional, I don't get too ruffled if someone declines an offer. My placements are guaranteed, so I'd prefer they decline than accept the offer and then quit a few months later. However, I do not want to be surprised by a decline. You can't close every search, but if you're totally caught by surprise when a candidate declines, you haven't been paying enough attention.

Victory! They Accepted!

Wahoo! They accepted! All your hard work paid off; you have a terrific person who is about to join your team.

So ... now what?

HOW TO

SET UP
YOUR NEW HIRE
FOR SUCCESS

Onboarding is the process a new employee moves through as they join your company. It starts the minute they walk through the door on their first day, and can last until the end of their first year of employment.

Hopefully, the candidate is as excited about their new opportunity as you are about adding them to your team. You want to keep their energy and enthusiasm high. This means being prepared and ready for them.

Depending on the position, here are some ways to make the onboarding experience successful:

⚡ Have a warm "meet and greet" with other team members (even if it's just you) to start the day. Consider a simple breakfast of coffee, orange juice, fruit salad, and pastries. A 15- to 30-minute event can break the ice.

⚡ Give them a tour of the office. Let them know where the bathroom is, where the office supplies are, where the coffee pot is, and let them know what others do for lunch, etc.

⚡ If they have a desk, make sure it's clean and stocked with the basic office supplies they will need. No one wants to start a new job at a desk full of the last person's crumbs and hair. YUCK.

⚡ If they will have a computer, make sure it's set up and ready to go with access to the network and printer. Have their email set up.

⚡ Let them know the specifics for their training. Depending on if it will be software or people-based, let them know what, when, and how they will be learning to do their new job.

INTERVIEWS AND OFFERS

chapter seventeen

When It Doesn't **WORK OUT**

Once you've thought about firing someone, it is really just a matter of time until you do it.

Gary Stauble
The Recruiting Lab

Firing people sucks.

Early in my career, I worked for a large regional specialty store. Part of my job as department manager, and then as HR manager, was to terminate people. It was mildly un-comfortable, but they had gotten their warnings — they should have known not to do it again. In my early career, I probably fired a dozen people. I didn't lose a ton of sleep over it and didn't think it was all that challenging.

Firing someone for "the man" is uncomfortable.

Firing someone when you are "the man" can be excruciating.

I know this by my own entrepreneurial hiring mistakes. I would sell them on me, the company, and the opportunity. I never stopped selling. **Don't make that mistake.**

However, if it's too late and you have some people on your team who are wonderful, but just not that great at the job you hired them for, own that you made a mistake in hiring them. I used to come up with a million excuses for why they weren't performing — I hadn't trained them enough, I hadn't given them enough resources, I wasn't good at holding them accountable. The list went on and on.

I also developed a bit of a "savior complex." I would start to feel like I was responsible for their mortgage, their car payment, and their daycare bills. If I didn't get them to succeed in this job — I was the failure. **Sounds crazy, right?** But, I would venture to guess if you have someone who isn't succeeding in your organization, these self-doubts have crossed your mind.

FIRING SUCKS,
PUTTING IT OFF JUST MAKES IT SUCK LONGER.

Re-Framing Firing

I truly believe everyone deserves a job they enjoy and are good at.

In recruiting, we are a performance-based business. Early in my entrepreneurial life, I would make excuse after excuse for people who weren't able to close deals. Finally, I realized: who wants a job they suck at? No one. So, if they can't admit that this is a bad fit for them, I will make that decision for them.

It's a lot easier to fire someone and feel okay about it when you know in your heart they'd be happier doing something else.

I believe it is crucial to keep the person in mind at the end of employment. This is someone you liked enough to hire and make part of your team. Make sure to be respectful and professional. You'd be surprised by how many people I have fired (or talked into quitting) that still invite me out for dinner and drinks. It doesn't have to be adversarial.

HIRE POWER

conclusion

CONCLUSION

Wahoo! You made it all the way to the end! I'm going to pat myself on the back for writing a book you found helpful enough to stick with to the end!

Thanks for letting me introduce you to the Hire Power Method.

My goal is for you to feel empowered, inspired, and in control.

If you like my style, and my approach, I'd love to help you and your business hire better. Please check out BuildingGurus.com or reach out to me at Rikka@BuildingGurus.com to learn about how I can support you.

Above all, don't forget…

Hiring is hard.

You won't get it right every time.

You may hire an amazing person who morphs into a disaster a year later.

You may get lucky and find a gem.

You may get screwed by a smooth talker.

You may start to doubt yourself.

But, no matter what happens, always remember …

Hiring is a game.

A complex, high-stakes game, but it's a game, nonetheless.

You're going to win some.

You're going to lose some.

The key to winning at this game is to always be learning.

What worked? What didn't?

What should I do again? What shouldn't I?

The good news is, you can't unlearn what you've learned by reading this book. You are bound to hire better for the rest of your life, because now you understand how the game is played. You will get better with every job ad, every interview, and every hire.

Now, you are in control.

You can find and hire the people you need to grow your business and achieve its true potential.

HIRE POWER

INSIDER INFO

DID YOU FIND THIS BOOK HELPFUL?

I truly hope so! If you did, please help others learn how they can start hiring better. The best way is by word of mouth to your friends, but another way can reach even more people who are struggling to find great people. If you write a simple Amazon review or LinkedIn recommendation you can help hundreds or perhaps thousands of other readers make their buying decision. With the information and encouragement, you can provide they can confidently take action. You can share anything you think will be useful, but here are a few ideas to get you started!

⚡ Why you decided to buy or read this book?

⚡ What did you like most about this book?

⚡ What makes this book different from others you have read?

⚡ Did it give you practical ways to apply the information it provides? If so, share what you are going to be doing differently because you read it.

⚡ What kinds of readers would benefit most reading this book?

The best time to leave a review is right after you've finished a book. So, now's the time if you want to help other LBM leaders and me!

HIRE POWER

About THE AUTHOR

Meet Rikka

I'm a bit of a freak of nature. I'll admit it.

I was **born** to be an entrepreneur — challenge, change, chaos, and excitement — sign me up!

I am **wired** to recruit — I love the strategy of search, the thrill of the hunt, the challenge of finding what a person is motivated by, and of course, I LOVE closing the deal.

I am crazy curious.

I love to learn.

Which is why I'm:

⚡ A licensed private pilot (licensed + retired in 2009)

⚡ A certified mind, body, spirit practitioner

⚡ A Universal Life minister (I've even done a baby blessing!)

⚡ I am a Landmark Forum graduate.

⚡ Certified in 5 of TTI's assessment sciences

I've spent well over $100,000 on trainings.

I love to learn and put my new knowledge to work.

But mostly,

I want to help LBM dealers and leaders get from where they are to where they want to be.

I want to take you from potential to profit through your people.

I am excited to educate you, empower you, and share my expertise with you so you can start to really believe that recruiting and retaining great people is a something you can learn and a game you can win.

Want
MORE?

I believe your recruiting and retention challenges can be solved one of 3 ways.

1. Education - when you know better, you do better. Check out my free and low cost trainings and workshops.

2. Empowerment - when you're ready to prioritize building a high performing team check out my Round Tables and Master Mind Groups.

3. Expertise - for critical and urgent key leadership positions with a compensation of over $100K check out my search services.

We're constantly evolving and updating our offerings, so check out BuildingGurus.com to see what's new and if you don't see something you're interested in just reach out to me at Rikka@BuildingGurus.com

 You can download your copy of the Hiring Toolkit, plus bonus resources for FREE at www.HirePowerBook.com/LBMtoolkit.

buildinggurus

www.BuildingGurus.com

HIRE POWER